Joe Penhall

Birthday

Methuen Drama

Published by Methuen Drama 2012

Methuen Drama, an imprint of Bloomsbury Publishing Plc

1 3 5 7 9 10 8 6 4 2

Methuen Drama
Bloomsbury Publishing Plc
50 Bedford Square
London WC1B 3DP
www.methuendrama.com

Birthday copyright © Joe Penhall 2012

Joe Penhall has asserted his rights under the Copyright, Designs
and Patents Act, 1988, to be identified as the author of this work

ISBN 978 1 408 17291 9

A CIP catalogue record for this book is available from the British Library

Available in the USA from Bloomsbury Academic & Professional,
175 Fifth Avenue/3rd Floor, New York, NY 10010.

Typeset by Mark Heslington Ltd, Scarborough, North Yorkshire
Printed and bound in Great Britain by
the MPG Books Group

ROYAL COURT

The Royal Court Theatre presents

BIRTHDAY

by **Joe Penhall**

BIRTHDAY was first performed at The Royal Court Jerwood Theatre Downstairs, Sloane Square, on Friday 22nd June 2012.

Principal Sponsor

BIRTHDAY

by Joe Penhall

(in order of appearance)
Ed **Stephen Mangan**
Lisa **Lisa Dillon**
Joyce **Llewella Gideon**
Natasha **Louise Brealey**

Director **Roger Michell**
Designer **Mark Thompson**
Lighting Designer **Hugh Vanstone**
Assistant Lighting Designer **Max Narula**
Sound Designer **John Leonard**
Casting Director **Amy Ball**
Assistant Director **Adele Thomas**
Production Manager **Paul Handley**
Stage Manager **Michael Dennis**
Deputy Stage Manager **Fran O'Donnell**
Assistant Stage Manager **Laura Sully**
Stage Management Work Placement **Bethany Sumner**
Costume Supervisor **Jackie Orton**
Voice Coach **Alan Woodhouse**
Dialect Coach **Tim Charrington**
Set Builders **Miraculous Engineering**
Set Painter **Kerry Jarrett**
Printing **Promptside**
Prosthetics **Paul Hyett**

The Royal Court and Stage Management wish to thank the following for their help with this production: Aid Call, Keir Bosley, B.Braun Medical Ltd, Coex-Hubris Ltd, Intersurgical Ltd, GE Healthcare, Mark Newman, The Whittington Hospital, Westminster Maternity Ward, May Westminster National Childbirth Trust, Dany & Wilder Dubois, Poppy & Noah Burton-Morgan, Gilly & Phil Clyde-Smith, Camilla Zervoglos, Johann Malawana, Sarah Savaskan, Vicki Scott, Norma Eros, Jenny Clearly, Friedericke Eben, Frances Lawrence.

THE COMPANY

JOE PENHALL (Writer)

FOR THE ROYAL COURT: Haunted Child, Dumb Show, Pale Horse, Some Voices.

OTHER THEATRE INCLUDES: Landscape with Weapon, Blue/Orange (National & West End); The Bullet (Donmar); Love and Understanding (Bush).

FILM INCLUDES: The Road, Enduring Love, Some Voices.

TV INCLUDES: Moses Jones, The Long Firm.

AWARDS INCLUDE: 2009 Best Screenplay at Roma Fiction Festival for Moses Jones, 2001 Olivier Award for Blue/Orange, Evening Standard Best Play Award for Blue/Orange, 2001 Critics' Circle Award Best New Play award for Blue Orange, 1995 Thames Television Best Play award for Pale Horse, 1995 John Whiting award for Some Voices.

LOUISE BREALEY (Natasha)

FOR THE ROYAL COURT: Behind the Image: Rough Cut, The Stone, Sliding with Suzanne (& UK tour).

OTHER THEATRE INCLUDES: Sixty-Six Books (Bush); Government Inspector (Young Vic); Country Music (West Yorkshire Playhouse); The Ones That Flutter (503); Pornography (Traverse Theatre/Birmingham Rep); Uncle Vanya (English Touring Theatre); Little Nell (Theatre Royal, Bath); After the End (Paines Plough/Brits Off Broadway); Arcadia (Bristol Old Vic).

FILM INCLUDES: The Best Exotic Marigold Hotel.

TV INCLUDES: Sherlock, Law & Order UK, Hotel Babylon, Mayo, Bleak House, Casualty.

RADIO INCLUDES: The Wall, Fair Stood the Wind for France, The Eggy Doylers, The Nine Days Queen, Pornography, The Ring and the Book, Have Your Cake, I Will Tell.

LISA DILLON (Lisa)

THEATRE INCLUDES: The Taming of the Shrew (RSC); Othello (RSC & West End); The Knot of the Heart, When the Rain Stops Falling, Period of Adjustment (Almeida); Hedda Gabler (Almeida & West End); Flea in Her Ear, Design for Living (Old Vic); Private Lives (Theatre Royal, Bath & West End); Under the Blue Sky, The Master Builder (West End); The Hour We Knew Nothing of Each Other, Present Laughter (National); The Cherry Orchard, Iphigenia (Crucible); As You Like It (Crucible/RSC).

FILM INCLUDES: Bright Young Things.

TV INCLUDES: The Jury II, Dirk Gently, Cranford, Hawking, Cambridge Spies.

RADIO INCLUDES: Something Wrong About the Mouth, Dr No, Howards End.

AWARDS INCLUDE: Ian Charleson Award Outstanding Newcomer 2004, Critics' Circle Most Promising Newcomer 2003.

LLEWELLA GIDEON (Joyce)

THEATRE INCLUDES: Running Dream (Albany); Bitter and Twisted (Black Theatre Co-op); Temporary Rupture (BTC); The Amen Corner, Blues Brother Soul Sisters (Bristol Old Vic); The Sunshine Boys (UK tour); Family Man, Big Life (Stratford East).

FILM INCLUDES: Different Girls, The Spice Girls' Spiceworld: The Movie, Manderlay, Nativity.

TV INCLUDES: Absolutely Fabulous, The Real McCoy, EastEnders, Holby City, Casualty, Murder Most Horrid, The Lenny Henry Show, TLC, Big Train, Porkpie, Doctors, The Crouches, Nighty Night, Bleak Old Shop of Stuff, English Express, Dani's House, Hotel Trubble, Bob the Builder.

RADIO INCLUDES: Clement Doesn't Live Here, Lenny Henry Easter Show, Behind the Couch, The Airport, The Emerald Green Show, The Little Big Woman Radio Show.

Llewella's writing credits include: Kerching, Smell the Purple, Fruit Salad, You Know Dem Way Deh, The Little Big Woman.

JOHN LEONARD (Sound Designer)

FOR THE ROYAL COURT: Tribes.

OTHER THEATRE INCLUDES: Detroit, Grief, Rocket to the Moon, London Assurance, The Power of Yes, England People Very Nice, Much Ado About Nothing, The Enchantment (National); Farewell to the Theatre, The Last of the Duchess, Skane, The Train Driver, Ecstasy (Hampstead); Filumena, The Master Builder, Becky Shaw, Measure for Measure, Rope, Waste, Duet for One, The Homecoming (Almeida); Ladies in Lavender, Basket Case (Royal & Derngate & UK tour); Here, The Lady from The Sea, The Snow Queen, As You Like It (Rose, Kingston); The Heresy of Love (RSC); Big Maggie (Druid & UK tour); The Cripple of Inishmaan, The Silver Tassie, The Gigli Concert, Long Day's Journey into Night, Leaves, Empress of India, The Druid Synge (Druid & Broadway & US tour); Beasts (503); Rattigan's Nijinsky, The Deep Blue Sea, The Master Builder (Chichester); Yes, Prime Minister, Cyrano de Bergerac, Calendar Girls, The Cherry Orchard, Taking Sides, Collaborations (Chichester & West End & tour); 5@50 (Royal Exchange); Takeaway and Ceiling/Sky (Stratford East); True West (Crucible); Restoration, A Month in the Country, People at Sea (Salisbury); The Glass Menagerie (The Gate, Dublin); Cool Hand Luke, Carrie's War, Duet for One, In Celebration, Kean, Donkey's Years, Summer and Smoke, Glengarry Glen Ross (West End); Translations (Princeton/Broadway).

AWARDS INCLUDE: Drama Desk Award, LDI Sound Designer of the Year, Fellow of the Guildhall School of Music & Drama, Honorary Fellow of the Hong Kong Academy of Performing Arts.

STEPHEN MANGAN (Ed)

FOR THE ROYAL COURT: The People are Friendly.

OTHER THEATRE INCLUDES: The Norman Conquests (Old Vic & Broadway); The Magic Carpet (Lyric Hammersmith); Noises Off (Piccadilly Theatre); A Midsummer Night's Dream, School for Scandal (RSC); She Stoops to Conquer (Birmingham Rep); As You Like It, Twelfth Night (Nottingham Playhouse); The Shoe Shop of Desire (Nottingham Playhouse/National); Hamlet (Theatre Royal, Norwich); Couch Grass & Ribbon (Watermill); The Rover (Salisbury); George Dandin, Mrs Warren's Profession (Redgrave Theatre); Much Ado About Nothing (Cheek By Jowl); Hayfever (Savoy).

FILM INCLUDES: Rush, An Act of Love, Cooked, War Wounds, Beyond the Pole, Someone Else, Confetti, Festival, Birthday Girl, Chunky Monkey, Billy Elliot, Martha Meets…, An Hour in Paradise.

TV INCLUDES: Episodes, Dirk Gently, The Hunt for Tony Blair, 10 Minute Tales, Free Agents, Never Better, Who Gets the Dog?, Miss Marple: At Bertram's Hotel, Green Wing, Jane Hall, Bromwell High, Nathan Barley, Ready When You are Mr McGill, I'm Alan Partridge, The Armando Iannucci Show, The Cappuccino Years, Sword of Honour, In Defence, Big Bad World, The Walker, Ditch the Bitch, Argumental, Lucky Jim, Party Political Broadcast.

RADIO INCLUDES: Number 10, Jack Rosenthal, Gordon Springer, Wilde Things, The Man Who Knew Everything, Into Exile, A Midsummer Night's Dream, As You Like It, And Another Thing…, Elvenquest, Baldi 5, The Black Cat Murder Mystery.

ROGER MICHELL (Director)

FOR THE ROYAL COURT: Tribes, My Night with Reg (& West End), The Key Tag, The Catch.

OTHER THEATRE INCLUDES: Rope (Almeida); Female of the Species (West End); Betrayal, Old Times (Donmar); Landscape with Weapon, Honour, The Homecoming, Under Milk Wood, The Coup (National); Blue/Orange (National & West End); Farewell to Theatre, Some Sunny Day (Hampstead); Some Americans Abroad (RSC & Lincoln Center, New York); Marya (Old Vic); Redevelopment, Restoration, Two Shakespearean Actors, Conversation, Kissing the Pope, The Constant Couple, Hamlet, Temptation, Merchant of Venice, The Dead Monkey (RSC); Macbeth (Nuffield, Southampton); The White Glove (Lyric Hammersmith); Private Dick (Lyric Hammersmith & West End); Romeo and Juliet (Young Vic); La Musica, Off the Top, Small Change (Brighton Actors Workshop).

FILM INCLUDES: Hyde Park on Hudson, Morning Glory, Venus, Enduring Love, The Mother, Notting Hill, Titanic Town, My Night with Reg, Persuasion.

TV INCLUDES: Buddha of Suburbia, Downtown Lagos, Ready When You are Mr Patel, Michael Redgrave, My Father.

AWARDS INCLUDE: Edinburgh Fringe First, Buzz Goodbody RSC Best Director Award, BAFTA, RTS Award, Evening Standard Award, Empire Award, Ecumenical Award, Emden, Best Director Reims International TV Festival, Best Film Seville Festival, Critics Circle Award, Locarno International Film Festival, Shanghai International Film Festival, Amanda Award (Norway).

He is a member of the Academy.

ADELE THOMAS (Assistant Director)

THEATRE INCLUDES: The Passion, The Passion: One Year On (National Theatre Wales/WildWorks); The Bloody Ballad (Theatr Iolo); Dog Days for Write Here (Traverse); No Vacancies, Deluge (Sherman Theatre); A Doll's House, The Legend of the Golden Swans (RWCMD); Under Milk Wood (Royal & Derngate); A Cold Spread (Chapter); Big Hopes (NT Connections); Bulletproof (Replay); Repeat (Dirty Protest); Sennedd (Welsh National Opera); The Good Soul of Szechwan (Young Vic TPR); An Enemy for the People (Sgript Cymru).

AWARDS INCLUDE: Regional Theatre Young Director Bursary.

MARK THOMPSON (Designer)

FOR THE ROYAL COURT: The Faith Machine, Tribes, Piano Forte, The Woman Before, Wild East, Mouth to Mouth, Six Degrees of Separation, Hysteria, The Kitchen, Neverland.

OTHER THEATRE INCLUDES: She Stoops to Conquer, One Man, Two Guvnors, London Assurance, England People Very Nice, The Rose Tattoo, The Alchemist, Once in a Lifetime, Henry IV Part I and II, The Duchess of Malfi, What the Butler Saw, Pericles, The Day I Stood Still, The Madness of George III, The Wind in the Willows (National); Life x3 (National/Old Vic & Broadway); Arcadia (National & Broadway); Measure for Measure, The Wizard of Oz, Much Ado About Nothing, The Comedy of Errors, Hamlet, The Unexpected Man (RSC); Insignificance, Company, The Front Page (Donmar); The Blue Room (Donmar & Broadway); Rope, Volpone, Betrayal, Party Time, Butterfly Kiss (Almeida); The Children's Hour, Female of the Species, Joseph & His Amazing Technicolor Dreamcoat, And Then There were None, The Lady in the Van, Dr Dolittle (West End); Follies (Broadway); La Bête, God of Carnage, Bombay Dreams, Art (West End & Broadway); Mamma Mia! (West End & Broadway & World tour); Blast (Hammersmith Apollo & Broadway); Kean (West End & UK tour); Funny Girl (Chichester).

OPERA & BALLET INCLUDES: The Mikado (Lyric Opera Chicago); Carmen (L'Opera Comique); Macbeth and Queen of Spades (Met Opera, New York); Falstaff (Scottish Opera); Peter Grimes (Opera

North); Ariadne auf Naxos (Salzburg); Il Viaggio a Reims (ROH); Hansel and Gretel (Sydney Opera House); The Two Widows (ENO); Montag Aus Licht (La Scala, Milan); Don Quixote (Royal Ballet).

FILM INCLUDES: The Madness of King George.

AWARDS INCLUDE: 4 Olivier Awards, 2 Critics' Circle Awards.

HUGH VANSTONE (Lighting Designer)

FOR THE ROYAL COURT: The Pain and the Itch; Mouth to Mouth (with Albery).

THEATRE INCLUDES: The Physicists, The Late Middle Classes (Donmar); Matilda (RSC & West End); Shrek (West End & US tour); Ghost, La Bête (West End & Broadway); The Wizard of Oz (West End & Toronto); Deathtrap (West End); The Real Thing (Old Vic); Arabian Nights (RSC); A Steady Rain (Broadway); Tanz Der Vampire (Berlin).

AWARDS INCLUDE: 3 Olivier Awards, Outer Critics Circle Award, Touring Broadway Award.

THE ENGLISH STAGE COMPANY
AT THE ROYAL COURT THEATRE

'For me the theatre is really a religion or way of life. You must decide what you feel the world is about and what you want to say about it, so that everything in the theatre you work in is saying the same thing ... A theatre must have a recognisable attitude. It will have one, whether you like it or not.'

George Devine, first artistic director of the English Stage Company: notes for an unwritten book.

photo: Stephen Cummiskey

As Britain's leading national company dedicated to new work, the Royal Court Theatre produces new plays of the highest quality, working with writers from all backgrounds, and addressing the problems and possibilities of our time.

'The Royal Court has been at the centre of British cultural life for the past 50 years, an engine room for new writing and constantly transforming the theatrical culture.' Stephen Daldry

Since its foundation in 1956, the Royal Court has presented premieres by almost every leading contemporary British playwright, from John Osborne's Look Back in Anger to Caryl Churchill's A Number and Tom Stoppard's Rock 'n' Roll. Just some of the other writers to have chosen the Royal Court to premiere their work include Edward Albee, John Arden, Richard Bean, Samuel Beckett, Edward Bond, Leo Butler, Jez Butterworth, Martin Crimp, Ariel Dorfman, Stella Feehily, Christopher Hampton, David Hare, Eugène Ionesco, Ann Jellicoe, Terry Johnson, Sarah Kane, David Mamet, Martin McDonagh, Conor McPherson, Joe Penhall, Lucy Prebble, Mark Ravenhill, Simon Stephens, Wole Soyinka, Polly Stenham, David Storey, debbie tucker green, Arnold Wesker and Roy Williams.

'It is risky to miss a production there.' Financial Times

In addition to its full-scale productions, the Royal Court also facilitates international work at a grass roots level, developing exchanges which bring young writers to Britain and sending British writers, actors and directors to work with artists around the world. The research and play development arm of the Royal Court Theatre, The Studio, finds the most exciting and diverse range of new voices in the UK. The Studio runs play-writing groups including the Young Writers Programme, Critical Mass for black, Asian and minority ethnic writers and the biennial Young Writers Festival. For further information, go to www.royalcourttheatre.com/playwriting/the-studio.

'Yes, the Royal Court is on a roll. Yes, Dominic Cooke has just the genius and kick that this venue needs... It's fist-bitingly exciting.' Independent

ROYAL COURT SUPPORTERS

The Royal Court is able to offer its unique playwriting and audience development programmes because of significant and longstanding partnerships with the organisations that support it.

Coutts is the Principal Sponsor of the Royal Court. The Genesis Foundation supports the Royal Court's work with International Playwrights. Theatre Local is sponsored by Bloomberg. The Jerwood Charitable Foundation supports new plays by playwrights through the Jerwood New Playwrights series. The Andrew Lloyd Webber Foundation supports the Royal Court's Studio, which aims to seek out, nurture and support emerging playwrights. Over the past ten years the BBC has supported the Gerald Chapman Fund for directors.

The Harold Pinter Playwright's Award is given annually by his widow, Lady Antonia Fraser, to support a new commission at the Royal Court.

PUBLIC FUNDING
Arts Council England, London
British Council
European Commission Representation in the UK

CHARITABLE DONATIONS
Martin Bowley Charitable Trust
Gerald Chapman Fund
City Bridge Trust
Cowley Charitable Trust
The Dorset Foundation
The John Ellerman Foundation
The Eranda Foundation
Genesis Foundation
J Paul Getty Jnr Charitable Trust
The Golden Bottle Trust
The Haberdashers' Company
Paul Hamlyn Foundation
Jerwood Charitable Foundation
Marina Kleinwort Charitable Trust
The Leathersellers' Company
The Andrew Lloyd Webber Foundation
John Lyon's Charity
The Andrew W Mellon Foundation
The David & Elaine Potter Foundation
Rose Foundation
Royal Victoria Hall Foundation
The Dr Mortimer & Theresa Sackler Foundation
John Thaw Foundation
The Vandervell Foundation
The Garfield Weston Foundation

CORPORATE SUPPORTERS & SPONSORS
BBC
Bloomberg
Coutts
Ecosse Films
Kudos Film & Television
MAC
Moët & Chandon
Oakley Capital Limited
Smythson of Bond Street
White Light Ltd

BUSINESS ASSOCIATES, MEMBERS & BENEFACTORS
Auerbach & Steele Opticians
Bank of America Merrill Lynch
Hugo Boss
Lazard
Louis Vuitton
Oberon Books
Peter Jones
Savills
Vanity Fair

DEVELOPMENT ADVOCATES
John Ayton MBE
Elizabeth Bandeen
Kinvara Balfour
Anthony Burton CBE
Piers Butler
Sindy Caplan
Sarah Chappatte
Cas Donald (Vice Chair)
Celeste Fenichel
Emma Marsh (Chair)
Deborah Shaw Marquardt (Vice Chair)
Sian Westerman
Nick Wheeler
Daniel Winterfeldt

 Supported by
ARTS COUNCIL ENGLAND

APPLAUDING
THE EXCEPTIONAL.

Coutts is proud to sponsor the Royal Court Theatre

Coutts | 👑

Joe Penhall

Birthday

For Ned, William and Emily Penhall

Characters

Ed, *thirties*
Lisa, *thirties*
Joyce, *Midwife, late thirties*
Natasha, *Registrar, late twenties*

The action takes place over several days in a modern NHS maternity hospital in London.

Act One

Scene One

5 p.m., Friday.

Ed *sits up in a hospital bed connected to a monitor.*

He is in mild pain, breathing hard.

We can hear the faint, intermittent screams of women in the background.

Lisa   You had a choice.

Ed   I know but my mind –

Lisa   I gave you the choice.

Ed   My mind was blown.

Lisa   We should have gone private.

Ed   I didn't think we could afford it.

Lisa   I told you I could.

Ed   We didn't the first time.

Lisa   I wasn't working then.

Ed   I was working.

Lisa   Sweetie, you're not paid what I'm paid.

Ed   Well I wasn't thinking straight.

Lisa   You went to all the classes, you knew what was going to happen, why didn't you bring it up before?

Ed   I was hormonal I couldn't get my head around – why are you laying into me?

Lisa   I'm not I'm just saying I gave you the choice I would have paid.

Ed   It's the same doctors.

Lisa   What doctors? We haven't even seen a doctor.

Ed   I didn't think it would be exactly –

Lisa   What did you think?

Ed   The same room overlooking the prison.

Lisa   That's not important.

Ed   I didn't think we could afford a private – it's exactly the same room as you had. That fucking prison . . .

Lisa   Oh well . . . it's only a prison you don't see it don't worry you don't see any, you know, *prisoners* . . .

Ed   I had you moved.

Lisa   Because it was cold not because of the –

Ed   Because it was cold *and* because of the prison. I made them move you.

Lisa   Let's just – you're just anxious – I understand – just calm down.

Ed   I'm trying – I'm trying to.

Lisa   Breathe. Deep breaths.

She holds his hand.

Take some gas.

She gives him gas.

Ed *takes several deep breaths.*

Lisa   Better?

He takes more gas.

Ed   Have you got the TENS machine?

Lisa   It's in your hospital bag.

Ed   Can you fish it out please?

She retrieves the TENS machine, starts unpacking it.

Did you get my raspberry leaf tea?

Lisa   Oh no. I forgot the tea.

Ed   You forgot? Fucking hell, Lisa. How could you forget my fucking raspberry leaf tea?

Lisa   I just had so many other things to do.

Ed   I need my raspberry leaf tea.

Lisa   Maybe I can go out and get you some.

Ed   I asked you to do one simple thing, buy a box of fucking tea . . . and you're so busy faffing around . . .

Lisa   I wasn't faffing around. You were faffing around with your hospital bag all morning . . .

Ed   I packed my hospital bag three nights ago while you were up all hours doing God knows what on the internet. What were you doing? Looking at porn?

Lisa   I wish.

Ed   All you had to do was order the TENS machine, buy some provisions and drive me here without crashing.

Lisa   We'll just get someone else to bring it.

Pause as she sets up the TENS machine.

Turn over.

He gets up on his haunches, back to her, she fits the TENS machine pads to his back as they talk.

Have you phoned your mum? Are they coming to see you?

Ed   No, they're not interested in any of this. They think it's just another of my stupid, you know, obsessions . . .

Lisa   I'm sure that's not the case.

Ed   You know it is. How many times have we seen them since I got pregnant?

Lisa   You need your mum.

Ed   Uh-huh . . .

Lisa   When I had Charlie my mum was the one who –

Ed   *I* was the one who –

Lisa   Well she was very supportive.

Ed   Wasn't I supportive?

Lisa   Of course but she's my mother.

Ed   That's better is it?

Lisa   She was able to understand.

Ed   She was 'able to understand' was she? The complexities? Because she's 'a woman'. And I'm just a quote unquote 'man' I suppose?

Lisa   Just – some people understand and some don't. You have to be prepared for that.

She finishes fitting the TENS machine pads.

She switches it on.

Tell me how this feels.

He winces.

Whoops sorry.

Ed   No it's fine, turn it up.

Lisa   Are you in pain?

Ed (*rearranging himself, trying to sit again*)   Yes no not really just uncomfortable.

Lisa   Wait till they start examining you.

Ed   What do you mean?

Lisa   All those fingers up you.

Ed   I'm having a caesarean.

Lisa I'm teasing.

Ed Don't even joke about it.

Lisa You won't feel a thing.

Ed I'm 'too posh to push'.

He gags.

Oh – I'm going to puke – can you get me a –?

She reaches for a bowl, hands it to him.

Lisa OK, get it all out now, you're doing fine . . .

Ed (*pointing*) There's some kitchen roll in the bag and I packed some antibacterial spray –

She retrieves the kitchen roll and spray.

Give the bowl a spray would you? And the cabinet. And the doorknob in the bathroom if you don't mind. (*Increasingly nauseous.*) And maybe the floor . . . you never know what germs are lurking . . .

She cleans.

He pauses over the bowl but nothing comes.

It's the nausea I can't handle. I'd rather have the pain.

Lisa No you wouldn't.

Ed Men can take the pain.

Lisa No you can't. That's just the myth they sell you.

Ed Beats morning sickness any day.

Lisa Don't talk to me about pain I had a breech.

Ed Don't talk about that now.

Lisa This won't be the same.

Ed That's why I'm here.

Lisa I didn't ask you to.

Ed   You couldn't do it again. There was no choice.

Lisa   Well there *was* – there was a choice – but –

Ed   An impossible choice. A terrible choice. It wasn't *even* a choice.

Silence.

He clutches his belly.

Ooh it's starting to hurt now.

Lisa   I'll turn it up.

She fiddles with the TENS machine controls.

I've forgotten how to do this. Is this OK? I don't want to cook you.

She turns it up, he nods, teeth gritted.

Ed   Do you think someone's coming?

Lisa   They'll come when something goes wrong.

Ed   What could go wrong?

Lisa   I don't know I'm just saying . . .

Ed   No don't start –

Lisa   With me –

Ed (*envisaging*)

Lisa   Nobody came until –

Ed   Don't worry me –

Lisa   It was an *emergency*.

Ed   What can go wrong? It's entirely different. That's the whole point.

Lisa   So they say.

Ed   What d'you mean?

Lisa   Being induced is no cakewalk.

Ed   It is for men.

Lisa   I doubt it.

Ed   I don't have to *dilate*.

Lisa   You're pumped full of hormones from arsehole to beak. You're bound to feel something.

Ed   Don't talk to me about hormones, I'm like a Bernard Matthews turkey. You don't know what I've been through with this; the tears the swollen ankles, you have no idea.

Lisa   Is that right?

Ed   The things I do for you.

Lisa   I did it for you.

Ed   But this is twice as hard.

Lisa   It's easier, it's obviously easier.

Ed   Well, I don't think it is now, I've changed my mind, I think that's just PR. I think the myth is that it's easier because if they told you how weird and unpleasant and unnatural it is nobody would do it. They have to sell it.

Lisa   Are you thirsty?

Ed   Photos on the website men like beach balls holding hands with proudly smiling women in business suits . . .

Lisa   Have some water, you'll get dehydrated.

Ed   Mum playing football with the kids while dad *gestates*. My father hates the idea . . .

Lisa (*pouring water from a plastic jug into a plastic cup*)   No, well, he's never really got it I suppose . . .

Ed   My entire family think it's daft and self-indulgent – we already have one, why fuck about with this? You didn't see the way they looked at me when I started showing – you didn't see –

Lisa   Who?

Ed   The neighbours, people in the street, people in shops.

Lisa   What are you talking about, it's nappy valley.

Ed   I took Charlie to the playground – six months pregnant – these milky Tory cows in their cashmere with their barren husbands with their Barbers and Bugaboos looking straight through me as if I'm not there – as if they personally *define parenthood* as if we're *transgressors*.

Lisa   Nobody can define parenthood. I can't even *describe* it half the time.

Ed   I can. It's the sharp end of the shitty stick.

Lisa   You don't mean that.

Ed (*pause, quietly*)   No, I don't. I'm going to say a lot of things I don't mean tonight. You'll have to bear with me.

Lisa   We're good parents.

Ed   Well I dearly wanted a girl and I have a right to a girl. Why shouldn't I have a go? I'm not self-indulgent, it's not as if I drive around in a Range Rover like half the fuckers in our street . . .

Lisa   Don't listen to the neighbours. They're just old-fashioned.

Ed   They're so Victorian and provincial!

Lisa (*handing him water*)   Here.

He sips anxiously, makes a face.

The water's horrible here, I remember that.

Ed   You'd think they'd sort it out. Is it clean?

Lisa   Of course it's clean it's just weird.

Ed   Everything tastes weird to me. I get one night out with my mates, one in – how many months? See a band – have my one unit of alcohol – can't even taste a curry properly.

Lisa   Poor baby.

Ed   They should put that on the posters. A man the size of a Volkswagen gagging over a curry. Nobody would do it.

Lisa   Just calm down.

Ed   I'm sorry I'm just feeling a bit –

Lisa   Stop panicking –

Ed   Delicate.

Lisa   Well just cheer up a bit.

Ed   You were an utter basket case when you had Charlie.

Lisa   Because –

Ed   Don't say it –

Lisa   Well it was very hard on me.

Ed   Hard on me too. An utter nutcase you. Raving at the midwife and imagining things.

Lisa   You just wait.

Ed   I'm not anticipating any –

Lisa   You'll see.

A midwife comes in, comes over, speaks quietly.

Joyce   Hello, I'm Joyce. I've just started my shift.

Ed   I'm Ed. Eddie.

Lisa   Lisa. Hi.

Joyce   Hi.

Ed   Hi.

Joyce   How's it going?

Lisa   Good.

Ed   Good.

Joyce   Good.

Joyce *takes the notes from the end of the bed, studies them.*

What time were you induced?

Lisa   Eleven o'clock this morning.

Joyce   And you came back at . . .?

Lisa   We went home to wait and then we came back at about four – he'd been in labour for about an hour.

Ed   We left it a bit late.

Lisa   We had plenty of time. There's no point in rushing they'll just send you home again.

Ed   I wanted to come back at three.

Lisa   Well, that's just you, isn't it?

Ed   I like to be early.

Lisa   It's better to be late.

Ed   But you don't understand how anxious it makes me feel.

Lisa   Just – will you – leave this to me. (*To* **Joyce**, *pointedly.*) They make such a fuss don't they?

Joyce   Oh yes, it's very strange for the men.

Joyce *places a hand on* **Ed**'s *belly.*

They take it all very seriously. (*To* **Ed**.) Don't worry. It's not the same as inducing a woman. We call it 'induction' but really it's just a way of getting things moving so the baby is in a good position for surgery.

Joyce *feels* **Ed**'s *belly in various places.*

Have they broken your waters yet?

Lisa   No we're still waiting.

Joyce   Well I think you're ready.

Lisa   Great, let's do it.

Ed   Hang on, I'm not sure I want my waters artificially broken.

Lisa   You don't want your artificial waters artificially broken?

Ed   It's not funny.

Lisa   Your artificial waters in your artificial womb.

Ed   Don't patronise me, Lisa.

Joyce   It'll speed things up.

Ed   It's just that I've heard about the risks . . .

Joyce   No, no. It's nice for men to break their waters.

Ed   Is it absolutely necessary?

Joyce   No, but it's liberating. It makes you feel like a woman.

Ed   I don't need to feel like a woman.

Joyce   Yes but you should, why not? It's good for you.

Ed   What are the risks? I've heard it can lead to complications –

Joyce   No I don't think so.

Ed   You don't *think* so? Well can you find somebody who *knows* so?

Joyce   There's a very small risk of complications if the waters are broken and the labour goes on a long time.

Lisa   You're having a bloody caesarean, what difference does it make?

Ed   The more procedures they do the more the complications.

Lisa   I think you're being a bit paranoid.

Ed   It's not part of my birth plan.

Lisa   I had my waters broken.

Ed   Yes but it's different with men. It's different!

Joyce   Oh, I don't think it really is.

Ed   What are you talking about? Of course it's different.

Lisa   Just listen to her Eddie. Don't be stubborn.

Ed   You're making it up as you go along. (*Pause, sighs*.) All right, let's just get on with it then.

Joyce   Good boy. You'll be out of here in no time.

She goes off to prepare a tray of instruments.

Ed   Will you please start supporting me here please?

Lisa   I am, I am supporting –

Ed   Just stop undermining me.

Lisa   What do you want me to say?

Ed   I want you to agree with me.

Joyce *returns.*

Lisa   He's getting quite uncomfortable now. Are you in a lot of pain?

Ed   Quite a bit actually.

Joyce   Good, things are moving then.

Ed   Moving?

Joyce   The baby has to move away from the bowel towards the abdominal cavity before we can operate, otherwise it's quite difficult to reach. Turn over please.

Ed   Where – on my?

Joyce   On your tummy.

Ed *turns over.*

And put your bottom in the air.

Ed   Why what are you going to do?

Joyce   You have a valve in your rectum which allows us to penetrate your womb through the bowel wall . . .

Ed *puts his bottom in the air hesitantly.*

The amniotic sac is possible to reach from here with – this is called an *amni-hook* – it might hurt a little but I'll try my best first to just . . .

Joyce *pulls on latex gloves with a snap,* **Ed** *braces himself.*

Loosen you up.

She produces a tube of KY jelly and slathers her hands, approaches **Ed**, *pushes fingers into his anus, selects a long thin instrument with a hook on the end – the amni-hook.*

She inserts the amni-hook.

Blackout.

Scene Two

7 p.m.

Ed *is sitting bolt upright, staring straight ahead, recovering from the procedure.*

Lisa *is standing staring out of the window at the rain.*

We can hear rain and the faint, intermittent screams of women – then a man – in the background.

The clock ticks.

Lisa   Whose idea was it to put a prison next to a maternity hospital? They're behind those windows now in ten-foot cells, wondering where their lives went, looking up at us behind our windows starting brand-new lives.

A loud dramatic alarm goes off outside the room.

Here we go.

She listens to various people and equipment going by the door.

Ed *still stares into space.*

Lisa *sits and picks up a newspaper, the* Guardian.

Have you seen this?

Ed *swivels slowly to look at her in disbelief.*

What are you looking at me like that for?

Ed (*sighs*)   What does it say?

Lisa   You probably shouldn't read it.

Ed   Just tell me.

Lisa   No it'll just upset you.

Ed   Just tell me.

Lisa   The head of the Royal College of Obstetricians says that if a man chooses to give birth in an NHS hospital he'll get less care on weekends and after hours.

Ed   It's always been like that.

Lisa   No, I thought the whole point was men are less work –

Ed   Caesareans aren't less work –

Lisa   Then they should get *more* care – even at weekends, surely . . .

She studies the paper.

Pause.

Ed   Well I don't know how they work it out.

Lisa   Maybe the time they save inducing –

Ed   It's obviously the time factor –

Lisa   And cutting them out –

Ed   Cutting's much quicker –

Lisa   They free up beds –

Ed   But – hang on – they need more doctors – they need a surgeon –

Lisa   And an anaesthetist –

Ed   Then I don't understand it.

Pause.

Lisa   I suppose if you're going to go around harvesting your wife's ovaries and transplanting embryos –

Ed   I think I'm allowed to harvest my own wife's ovaries!

Lisa   Then as far as they're concerned you're asking for trouble. What do you expect?

Ed   They just don't like it because there's more to go wrong.

Lisa   A lot can go wrong with any birth.

Ed   What's to go wrong? There's nothing wrong with me. Stop *worrying* me.

Pause.

She studies paper, thinks.

Lisa   But they gave you the *choice* when to be induced – they asked you today or Monday? And you said today.

Ed   *You* said today.

Lisa   Because it's better for me on a Friday.

Ed   Well it's not Friday any more now it's Friday night now –

Lisa   I didn't know it would take so long –

Ed   You'd think they'd tell us it can take this long before we choose – they don't tell you *anything*. You'd think we'd be *informed* – I want to be *informed* – 'informed consent' – in what way am I giving . . .?

Lisa   They were very kind and gentle and patient with you when you got your embryo. They were fine when they took my –

Ed   Yes well as taxpayers we have a right to –

Lisa   It was so easy –

Ed   A certain standard of care. I pay a lot of tax so I'll be looked after when I go into hospital.

Lisa   *I* pay a lot of tax.

Ed   OK *you* pay a lot of tax so I'll be looked after –

Lisa   I worked my tits off so you could take maternity leave –

Ed   And I'm grateful – don't make me feel guilty –

Lisa   Well you just –

Ed   What?

Lisa   You take it for granted sometimes.

Ed   You take me for granted.

Lisa   I had a laparoscopy for you.

Ed   Only because we had to. We had no choice.

Lisa   Please don't say that, you have no idea how much that upsets me.

Ed   It upsets me too.

Lisa   Well it upsets me more so just put a bloody sock in it. We did what we did, we did what we had to do, let's just get her out now and get on with our lives.

Pause.

She picks up the newspaper, reads.

There's obviously certain things they don't want to get into because, you know, there isn't the time and people probably wouldn't do it if they knew absolutely everything.

Ed   That's how they get away with it, they get away with
lack of care and poor standards and infections and short
staffing – they don't care if you have a terrible experience
because you don't want to talk about it and the chances are
you won't be back anyway. You might come back in a few
years – by which time you've forgotten.

Lisa   Women are probably *programmed* to forget – or
brainwashed – it's a whole Darwinian – it's an evolutionary
tool – but men? Who knows what men do? You may never
get over it.

He suddenly lets out a loud groan.

She leans over, finds the gas mask, hands it to him, he sucks on it.

Deep breaths, that's the way. Keep hold of it and just keep
. . . pretend it's a joint.

He takes big breaths, then offers it.

Ed   You want some?

Lisa   No I can't be bothered.

Ed   It's pretty useless really I'd rather smoke a joint.

Lisa   I don't think they'll let you in here.

*She presses the call button and it can be heard sounding in
the distance.*

They'll leave you dangling for as long as possible. That's
what happened to me. They should at least give you
pethidine.

She returns to reading the paper.

Pause.

He watches her reading the Guardian *enviously.*

Ed   The *Guardian* . . . What a load of wankers . . .
they're just fearmongering . . . The *Daily Mail* for
handwringing liberals . . .

Pause.

What else does it say?

Lisa   Says you'll have inexperienced junior doctors performing the caesarean.

Ed   Well, that's just rationalism. That's obviously how they can afford – hold the front page: 'Young doctors allowed to work in hospitals – shock horror.'

Silence.

Ed *sighs, grunts, tired.*

Lisa   How are you feeling?

Ed   Tired. How long do I have to sit here like this?

Lisa   It should be just a few hours.

Ed (*checking clock*)   It's been two hours since they broke my waters.

Lisa   Well she's just getting ready in her own sweet time. (*Intones to his belly.*) Come on little baby, come on sweetie, time to come out now, we're ready for you. Tell her to come out Ed.

Ed   Happy birthday . . . time's up . . . time to come out now little one.

They wait.

Come out!

Pause.

Not a sausage, must be asleep. Really hasn't moved at all as far as I can tell, I hope she's all right.

Lisa   Charlie was like that, quiet inside, rowdy as all hell when he got out.

Ed   I never feel her kick. Have a feel.

Lisa *feels his belly, frowns slightly.*

My balls are like coconuts.

Lisa   Really? That's interesting.

Ed   I've had the most enormous erection for the past hour. It's like a cricket bat.

Lisa   When the placenta rubs against the prostate gland it can be very sexually stimulating, or so they say, I wouldn't know about that . . .

Ed   I wouldn't go that far, it's actually very uncomfortable.

He feels his erection under the covers.

Lisa   You want me to . . .?

Ed   What?

Lisa   Well I could probably . . .

She looks around, as if somebody might come in.

Ed   What . . .?

Lisa   Just gently . . . Give you a quick . . . (*She gestures, mouths it, 'wank'.*)

Ed   . . .? (*Mouths it, 'a wank?'*)

Lisa   Quick one . . .

Ed   For God's sake . . . it's about the furthest thing from my mind!

Lisa   Really?

Ed   You know how I feel about sex at the moment.

Lisa   No I don't.

Ed   I blow hot and cold.

Lisa   All right. I'm only trying to help.

Ed   It's all you ever think about. (*Pause, quietly.*) You could suck me off in the bathroom if you like. Might as well, if you're going to start all that again.

Lisa   Don't be silly . . . (*Eyeing bathroom door.*) It's too small.

Ed   Well don't offer to, you know . . .

Lisa   I was just being spontaneous.

Ed   It sends out the wrong signals.

Lisa (*pause, quietly*)   When *I* was pregnant we did it all the time – did it the night before I went into labour.

Ed   I was trying to bring it on. Tried everything. Tweaked the nipples. Finger up the bum. Pineapples. All very weird. It's amazing some of the advice you get on the NHS.

Lisa   We managed.

Ed   I managed all sorts of things *then* – cunnilingus at nine months everything in the wrong place not a million laughs but we got there in the end . . . you wore kitten heels and a ra-ra skirt.

Lisa   You don't even try now.

Ed   Do you want me to wear kitten heels and a ra-ra skirt?

Lisa   Why don't you try?

Ed   It's embarrassing.

Lisa   That's why I offered to just –

Ed   No no no no. It's all or nothing with me. Feast or famine. Just get the midwife back here, I need a painkiller.

Lisa   What can you feel?

Ed   A sore arse.

She leans over and presses the call button. She gives him a quick kiss on the forehead.

Lisa   Now you know.

Ed   Now I know what? What it's like to have somebody's fingers up my arse? When have you had somebody's fingers up your arse?

She gives him a look.

Don't answer that – I'm not in the mood. I thought I was going to shit myself again. It's not the same for a man, shitting oneself . . .

Lisa   Why?

Ed   It's just more natural for women . . . for all sorts of funny reasons . . .

Lisa   Tell me the funny reasons. Tell me the funniest of the funny reasons.

Ed (*thinks, cogs whirring*)   I don't know what I'm talking about. I'm gassed out of my mind, I'm allowed to say things like this. Just help me do my relaxation technique.

She comes closer, holds his hands in hers.

Lisa (*intones calmly*)   Three . . . two . . . one . . . relax . . .

He takes a deep breath.

Three . . . two . . . one . . . relax . . .

He lets out his breath.

An alarm on the monitor starts beeping.

Ed   Here we go.

Lisa   You probably just moved.

She has a fiddle with the monitor on his belly.

I think that's OK.

Ed   How can you be sure?

She presses the call button again.

They wait as it sounds in the distance.

I'm sure you're probably right . . . but we can't be sure . . .

Lisa   When I had Charlie –

Ed   This is totally different –

Lisa   It's not really that different –

Ed   It's completely different, are you mad?

Lisa   I don't honestly think the heart rate is dropping to . . .

They stare at the dropping heart rate on the monitor, unsure what to do.

Pause.

Ed   Well I want to see the midwife now just to set my mind at ease.

Lisa *fiddles around with the monitor strapped to his belly again.*

Lisa   Wait, lift your bum.

Ed   No get the midwife –

Lisa   I can do it –

Ed   I don't want you to do it –

Lisa   Why?

Ed   Because you're not qualified! Just wait –

Lisa   You'll be waiting all night.

Ed   It's *her* job, she should do her job – is it too much to ask? That they do their jobs so we don't have to?

Lisa   You had the choice to go private.

Ed   Don't blame me for this – you're always blaming me.

Lisa   I'm not I just want you to be comfortable.

Ed   I'll be comfortable if they switch that alarm off.

Lisa   Just let me do it, lift your bum.

Ed   No. It's the principle.

He presses the call button again.

Pause.

Ed *sighs, lifts up,* **Lisa** *fiddles with the straps, repositions the monitor on his belly.*

The alarm stops.

Joyce *comes in.*

Joyce   Hello. How's it all going?

Ed   Why does that alarm keep going off?

Joyce   I expect it just slipped off you.

She repositions the monitor on him.

Lisa   He needs a painkiller.

Ed   I want an epidural.

Lisa   Is that possible?

Joyce   Have you been induced?

Lisa   Yes this morning.

Joyce   Are you in pain?

Ed   Can't you tell?

Joyce   It means the baby's coming – it's good.

Lisa   Are you going to examine him?

Joyce   Yes yes soon.

Lisa   Well when?

Joyce   I'll come back in a minute.

Lisa   A minute?

Joyce (*leaving*)   Yes I won't be long. Don't worry.

She goes.

The clock ticks.

Pause.

Ed   It always worries me when they say don't worry.

Lisa   They're obviously very busy tonight.

He groans.

Three . . . two . . . one . . . relax . . .

Ed   Oh, I have a very, very bad feeling about this.

Lisa   Shh, it'll be good for you, it'll make a man of you.

Lights down.

Scene Three

10 p.m.

In the blackout – **Ed** *is moaning in pain, long, loud labour moans.*

Lights up on – **Lisa** *sitting beside him on the bed, holding his hand.*

Lisa   You're doing really well, I'm really proud of you.

He keeps moaning.

Ed   When will they examine me?

Lisa   I don't know. They should soon.

Ed   She could have the cord around her neck –

Lisa   She won't have the cord around her neck –

Ed   Charlie had the cord around his neck –

Lisa   I suppose they should examine you just in case –

Ed   Call them in.

Lisa   I've called, I've called about three times –

Ed   I feel so sick it's like my worst ever hangover plus gastroenteritis.

Lisa   That's good.

Ed   Why is it good?

Lisa   It's definitely on its way. Are you going to be sick?

She gets the bowl.

Ed   No just get me some water . . .

She pours more water, holds it to his lips.

Thanks . . .

Lisa   You're doing really, really well.

Ed   Uh, it's so boring!

Lisa   Not long now . . .

Ed   I'm so hot – is it hot in here?

Lisa   No it's cold actually.

She goes to the bathroom and wets a flannel.

Ed   I'd kill for a beer. Two units a week? That's not even a Budweiser.

Lisa (*off*)   It's a pint, that's enough.

Ed   One pint a week? With all this to contend with? My nerves are in shreds.

Lisa (*returning*)   It's done you good you look great.

Ed   Thank you.

Lisa   Glowing – it suits you. (*Mopping his brow and lips.*) As long as you let me go back to work again . . .

Ed   After your paternity leave absolutely – two weeks you said – you promised me.

Lisa (*patting him*)   Don't worry I won't make you do it all on your own.

Joyce *comes in and comes over.*

Joyce   Hello, how are we doing? Have you been induced?

Ed   Yes yes I was induced this morning!

Joyce   Well I think you're well on your way now.

Ed   Please I'm in a lot of pain I need an epidural.

Joyce   Oh, you shouldn't be.

Ed   Well I am.

Joyce   It's not so bad for a man.

Ed It is for me.

Joyce No it's really not necessary. You're not having contractions. You won't need an epidural.

Ed I will if you keep shoving things up me.

Joyce Sometimes it's good to hang on for as long as you can.

Ed I have – I am.

Joyce You're nearly there.

Ed *looks at* **Lisa** *for help.*

Lisa He has a great deal of abdominal pain and is obviously very uncomfortable.

Joyce *feels* **Ed**'s *belly.*

Joyce Mm. Normally the stomach moves upwards to make room for the baby but yours has not moved. You have a lot of belly fat. Do you drink a lot of beer?

Ed I have the odd glass of wine . . .

Joyce You need to lose weight. This could be the reason the baby is not moving . . .

She feels his belly and sides.

The baby is wedged between your bowel wall and your belly. You need to lose a stone in weight.

Ed *Now?*

Joyce If you have been induced it should move more quickly than this.

Ed *groans.*

Lisa When I was induced I was strongly advised to have an epidural.

Joyce We don't give epidurals to men.

Lisa   Well he needs a painkiller of some sort.

Joyce   Are you using gas and air?

Ed   It's like sucking the air out of an old bicycle tyre. My mouth is like Velcro.

Lisa   What else can you give him?

Joyce   Let me take his temperature.

She gets out a thermometer.

Ed   What are you going to do with that?

Joyce   I'm going to put it in your mouth.

She puts it under his tongue.

I can give him pethidine but it's not ideal.

Ed   Yes – give it – give it!

Joyce   There is a small risk it could cross the placenta.

Ed   Uh . . .

Lisa   How do you feel about that?

Ed   I don't care – anything!

Joyce   Or you could try some Panadol. I have some somewhere.

Ed   *Panadol?*

Joyce   Let's see what his temperature is and then you can decide.

They wait a moment.

Lisa *holds his hand.*

Lisa   One . . . two . . . three . . .

Ed   Three two one three two one!

Lisa   Sorry –

Ed Both hands –

Lisa (*takes both hands*)   Three . . . two . . . one . . . relax . . .

Ed Turn up the TENS machine, where's the fucking TENS machine?

Lisa It's all twisted up.

Lisa *untwists the TENS machine laboriously.*

Joyce *removes the thermometer and reads it.*

Joyce I'll get you a saline drip for the dehydration.

Ed Just give me the pethidine.

Joyce You have a slight temperature – I should try with Panadol first.

She sets up a saline drip on a stand.

Ed I'm just hot because I've been sitting here for hours and hours wracked with pain the window doesn't open I've had nothing to drink I need a cold drink and a sandwich – ow that really . . .

She is inserting an IV needle into his arm, connecting it to the drip.

Lisa I'll get you a sandwich and a Ribena in a minute, don't worry.

Ed I need a beer – an ice-cold beer – a Pils – or large brandy – I haven't had a proper drink in nine months – it's inhuman.

Joyce Tsk!

Joyce *produces Panadol.*

I'll give you the Panadol and you can see how you get on.

Ed Panadol doesn't work on me.

Joyce We'll try this first and if it doesn't work we can try something else.

Ed   You'll give me pethidine?

Joyce   Try this first.

Ed   All right but give me a few.

Joyce   Uh?

Ed   Give me a few; three or four it usually takes, you know, for a headache or, or . . .

He watches as she breaks out a Panadol suppository, takes off the monitor strapped to his belly, rearranges his nightgown.

Joyce   Turn over.

Ed   Why?

Joyce   It's a suppository.

Ed   Why can't I have it orally?

Joyce   This is faster. Just turn over please.

Ed   Why can't I have an epidural? What are they hiding? Why do you keep going out of the room? What's really going on here?

Lisa   Ed cool it please. (*To* **Joyce**.) I'm sorry. When are you going to operate? We've been waiting since four o'clock!

Joyce   The anaesthetist is very busy tonight.

Lisa   Busy where, why? I'm sorry but you understand –

Joyce   I just called for him and I just missed him, I'm sorry, he just went into emergency theatre a minute ago –

Lisa   Well I'm sorry but –

Joyce   I'm sorry –

Lisa (*simultaneous*)   No I'm sorry –

Joyce (*simultaneous*)   I'm sorry –

Lisa   But I really think we really need him here now –

Joyce   It's just one of those things, if I'd made the call two minutes earlier . . .

Lisa   I asked you two hours ago.

Joyce   It's really very common, it's nothing to worry about, he'll come to you as soon as he's finished.

Lisa   When will he finish?

Joyce   I don't know, he won't be long.

Ed   How long, an hour, two hours?

Joyce   Oh I should think about an hour, you know he's very busy . . .

Ed   And there's no other anaesthetist?

Joyce   We'll have another one on Monday.

Ed   This is exactly what happened when Charlie was born!

Lisa   Eddie please be quiet – do what you're told for God's sake you're just making it worse – take some gas and air.

Ed   You don't understand, it's my body.

She plugs the gas to his mouth.

Lisa   Deep breaths, that's it.

He calms down a bit.

Joyce   Can you please turn over now?

Ed   Couldn't I just have another drip?

Joyce   You already have saline, it's enough for now.

Ed   I need to shit.

Joyce   That's quite normal. The baby is pushing on your bowel – she wants to come out.

Ed   She's barking up the wrong tree there then.

Joyce   Turn over now.

He sighs, turns over.

On your side.

He lies on his side, she inserts the suppository.

Ed   You're quite rough, aren't you? Has anyone ever told you that? Like changing a lightbulb.

Joyce   It's never as easy as you think.

Ed   No kidding. I've been fingered more times than an unripe avocado.

He rolls over and sits up.

Joyce *turns away to clear up, leaving* **Ed** *uncovered.*

Ed *lies on his side.*

If I'd known I couldn't have an epidural . . . they don't tell you that.

Lisa   You're not having *contractions* – she just *said* – you're not listening.

Ed   All right – yes – I know – I'll try, shall I? I'll try and have a *contraction* for you, shall I? Call a gynaecologist I'm going to *dilate*. Just to keep the women happy.

He grunts and strains theatrically throughout the next few lines.

Lisa   Perhaps you should give him a scan.

Joyce   He seems fine.

Lisa   Well I don't think it's moving. You haven't checked the position for a while.

Joyce   I'll come back in a few minutes and examine him.

Lisa   Can't you do it now while he's all ready for you? (*To* **Ed**.) What are you doing?

Ed (*straining*)   I'm locating my inner vagina. What does it look like?

Joyce   I'll come back later.

Lisa   What are you going off to do?

Joyce   I have all sorts of things to do.

Lisa   I really think he needs –

Joyce   Yes all right in a minute –

Lisa   No you listen to me: my husband has told you he's in terrible pain. He's asked for pethidine and I'm asking you to examine him – I've done this before and I'm not going to argue. That's my position.

Pause.

Joyce   I just have this emergency to deal with and I'll come straight back to you, don't worry.

Lisa   Right now. Please. (*Beat.*) Thank you. (*Beat.*) I'm tired of arguing. (*Beat.*) Can you hear me when I speak to you?

Joyce *smiles and goes out.*

Ed   They don't give a fuck, do they? Is she on drugs? She's half asleep.

Lisa   No, just not very bright, lazy cow.

Ed   Maybe it's a cultural thing. Maybe where she comes from it's just an entirely different approach to childbirth?

Lisa   Maybe she just doesn't like men having babies. It's probably against her religion. I hope she's not some sort of Christian fundamentalist or a Muslim.

Ed   No, Muslims love it. When I walk past the mosque on Uxbridge Road I always get a cheer. The men in the cab office are always so kind to me. They really make a fuss of me.

Lisa   She's just tired probably.

Ed   Well I wish she wouldn't take it out on me.

Lisa *covers* **Ed** *up and helps him turn around and resume his original sitting position.*

Lisa   Don't worry. I'll look after you. There you go. You're doing really fantastically well there, sweetie pie . . .

She pats and strokes his head.

You're being very brave.

Ed   I'm starving. What have we got to eat?

Lisa   I've got a banana in my bag.

Ed   Just the one? One banana?

Lisa   I didn't think we'd be here so long. It's so much faster with men.

Ed   How long have we been here?

Lisa   Hours! It's four hours since they broke your waters.

Ed   For God's sake, four? Charlie only took five. I don't know why I've bothered.

Lisa   You know why.

She rummages in her bag.

She hands him the banana, he just stares at it.

Ed   No no no, I'm in no condition to eat a banana.

He puts the banana on the table.

Lisa   I've got some crisps.

Ed   Not allowed. They need to operate on an empty stomach.

Lisa   I'll have them.

She produces crisps, opens them, eats one.

Ed   Oh no, no. You'll get crumbs everywhere. I'm trying to keep the place clean . . .

He picks up the spray and kitchen roll and wipes the table.

Lisa *puts away crisps.*

Did you bring my magazines?

Lisa　No because I didn't think we'd be here this long.

Ed　Lisa! I need my magazines! There's a diet I want to look at . . . I need distractions . . . I can't go through what you went through with Charlie, I really can't. The whole thing was a nightmare from start to finish.

Lisa　Don't say that. And don't call it a 'nightmare'. I can't think like that –

Ed　Why can't you?

Lisa　Because it makes me feel like a victim.

Ed　We both are. You haven't seen what I've seen. People with their fists right up you to the elbow.

Lisa　I'm glad I didn't see it.

Ed　Sewing you up, cuts, cutting, blood gushing –

Lisa　I've forgotten all about it.

Ed　Well I haven't. Like a shark attack. It's worse for the man.

Lisa　Oh poor you!

Ed　You didn't have to stand there listening to the ear-splitting screams while one congenital fuckwit after another came in, rummaged around inside you and then fucked off for a smoke. No epidural. No doctors. You didn't see them at the end, stitching you back together, legs akimbo, marinating in your own blood and shit, great strings of blood like drool. I don't know why they invited me to watch – why do they do that? They kept showing me your vagina as if it were a *holy relic*. (*Staring into space.*) Men are visually stimulated. It's our worst nightmare. Suddenly this blissful, heavenly organ, this ravishing *jewel* you've been obsessively petting and tending and eyeing with rapture all those years becomes the most alarming, harrowing thing you've ever seen in your life! It's a wonder I'm not completely *gay* by now. Because I'm telling you, as a man, once you've had a child, once you've watched a *live human* emerge from your wife's vagina, by God you need a change of scenery.

Lisa   Oh shut up, Eddie. Just pull yourself together.

Ed   He was blue when he came out. Midnight blue and rubbery as a rubber chicken – you didn't even see it.

Lisa   It happens all the time, it's normal.

Ed   He nearly died about three times.

Lisa   And they brought him back and he's a beautiful little boy and I got over it and we're all fine now.

Ed   Well you didn't because –

Lisa   All right.

Ed   You were mutilated.

Silence.

And so now it's all *this*. God knows why I thought this would be different. I must be out of my mind.

Silence.

Lisa   I didn't realise you were so traumatised. You could have had counselling.

Ed   Could I? Nobody offered.

Lisa   Well we could have found somebody.

Ed   And paid for it. Paid because they traumatised us both so much.

Lisa (*sighs*)   The real trouble started later if you really want to know . . . all that silly business when he went off me, kicking me and complaining whenever I came into the room.

Ed   He was traumatised too.

Lisa   Well I don't think we ever got back to normal – I don't think we ever got over that –

Ed   You probably didn't.

Lisa   Well doesn't that make you sad? It's the only thing I regret. My relationship with him is so intense and fraught now – because I've always felt I had to compensate for the –

Ed   For the birth –

Lisa   Yes and compensating for all the miscarriages.

Ed   All right look I think we're being a little bit –

Lisa   What?

Ed   Melodramatic. We're pathologising the boy when really he's fine. When he gets his little sister – when he has a *sibling* . . . it's going to be great fun . . .

Lisa   I just want to be a proper mother and not have to worry about all this. I just want everything to be OK with Charlie – with my little boy again. Because it's really upset me I don't think you realise Ed. To be honest . . . it's broken my heart.

Pause.

Ed   Maybe if you weren't away on business all the time worrying about your career . . .

Lisa   Don't *turn* on me, we're just turning on each other now, we're like veal in a crate . . .

Ed   I have a right to choose this for *myself*. A basic right to experience childbirth for myself.

Lisa   A *right*?

Ed   Has it occurred to you I might *enjoy* it?

Lisa   Now you feel *entitled* to it? First you felt entitled to give childbirth a *miss* and let me get on with it – *now* you're an *Earth Mother*.

Ed   Yes I am – and I'm good at it, frankly –

Lisa   So it's about *entitlement*.

Ed   We had no choice –

Lisa   We had a choice but a pretty grim one –

Ed   And I wanted a girl –

Lisa   Because you wanted another child, you wanted a *girl* and so you chose a girl embryo and went through the whole procedure and now it's all *this*.

Pause.

Ed   Well – thank you.

Lisa   All right.

Ed   No I mean it. Thank you. For giving me the opportunity and going back to work and all the rest of it I know it's not easy.

Lisa   Working?

Ed   Being the breadwinner.

Lisa   Are you kidding? Easier than bringing up children all day every day. Easier than arguing with you all day and night about nappies and kiddy meals and buggies. Sitting in my own office, a view of the river, fresh coffee, lunches, people telling me how clever I am all day? It's a fucking cakewalk.

Ed   You're just saying that to make me feel better.

Lisa   No I mean it, it's much easier being the man, being the woman sucks.

Ed   It's a lot of responsibility.

Lisa (*patting him*)   Just don't worry your pretty little head about it.

Lights down.

Scene Four

2 a.m. Saturday.

Ed *is on his hands and knees on the bed, sweating, feverish, quietly grunting and trying to move.*

Lisa *is slouched in the chair, jacket off and draped over herself for warmth, head down, snoozing.*

The clock ticks . . .

Ed *lets out a moan and* **Lisa** *wakes up.*

Lisa   What's happening? What can I do?

Ed   I just think I'm in the wrong position – if I was in a different position the suppository might –

Lisa   It's not going to move –

Ed   It's not working, if I was in a different position – I don't know – oh I just want it to hurry up now.

Lisa   I'll help you move.

Ed   I feel like I'm being fucked by a donkey.

Lisa   Now you know.

Ed   Stop saying that. When have you been fucked by a donkey?

She gets up and helps him, she rearranges his gown and the monitor.

Lisa   Whoops, showing a bit of flank there . . .

Ed   Don't it's cold . . .

Lisa   I'm covering you up.

Ed   You're having a good look.

Lisa   Trust me, there's nothing up there I need to see.

Ed   Look at me; my breasts are like udders – if I have to swallow any more hormones I'll turn into a ladyboy.

Lisa Just try and get comfortable.

Ed When did I ask for pethidine? Hours and hours ago. It's a scam. Now I understand – they only do men to save money on painkillers. It saves time, saves beds . . . well? Am I right?

Lisa I doubt it.

He grunts as he changes position.

Joyce *comes in and fiddles with the tap on the drip in his arm.*

Ed Ow, what are you doing?

Joyce I'm trying to take this out now but it's just stuck –

Ed Ow!

Lisa What's wrong?

Joyce I must have tied it too tight . . .

She keeps yanking it to no avail.

Oh dear . . .

She tries with forceps to dislodge the tap but eventually gives up.

I guess I don't know my own strength.

Ed *stares at his arm in disbelief, rubs it.*

Lisa Where is the anaesthetist?

Joyce (*as if it's fresh news*) Actually the anaesthetist has just gone into theatre to deal with an emergency.

Lisa (*sighs*) How much longer will he be?

Joyce I really don't know. Who knows?

Lisa Well somebody must know.

Joyce They'll have a lot of stitching to do and then they have to write up their notes – it's very important they write up their notes – they cannot be interrupted.

Ed   Just ask them how long, how long will it take?

Joyce   Nobody knows these things.

Lisa   No no no no you listen to me – when I do my job and somebody asks me how long it's going to take *I fucking know*. OK? I'm *paid* to *know*. Because I'm a *professional*.

Pause.

Joyce   Maybe an hour, maybe two. Have you been induced?

Lisa (*to* **Ed**)   I'm going to go bananas in a minute.

Joyce   Are you still in pain?

Lisa   Yes – he is – what language do you want it in?

Joyce   You've already had a painkiller.

Lisa   It didn't work obviously.

Joyce   Do you need to go to the toilet?

Ed   No thanks.

Joyce   If you have a full bladder it creates extra pressure. Perhaps if you go to the toilet . . .

He tries to move but the drip and the monitor impede him.

Ed   How am I supposed to do that? I'm a walking laboratory.

Joyce   Just go anyway. See how it feels.

Ed   Now? Here?

Joyce   Yes yes go on. It's nice.

He tries to urinate.

Ed   No no this is – I can't do this . . .

Joyce   Try.

Ed   I'm shy.

Lisa   Is there a bedpan?

Ed   I can't do it with an audience. Men can't do it with an audience, everybody knows that.

Lisa *just rubs her eyes.*

Joyce   I'll give you a catheter to drain your bladder and if you still don't feel better I'll try and find you some pethidine.

Ed   A catheter?

Joyce *produces a catheter.*

Where are you going to put that?

Lisa   Where do you think?

Ed   No I beg you.

Joyce   Usually it does the trick.

Ed (*trying to get up*)   I'll have a piss I'll piss I'll piss for all I'm worth . . .

Joyce   Just hold still please . . .

Ed   I've changed my mind . . . I'm fine, really . . .

Joyce   I want to make sure you have an empty bladder.

She rummages around under the blankets.

Ed *clenches his fists and teeth as she inserts the catheter.*

Lisa *watches, appalled.*

Lisa (*pause*)   I had to have a catheter. I wouldn't wish it on my worst enemy.

Joyce   How does that feel?

He stares in disbelief.

Joyce *drains his bladder.*

There it is. How do you feel now? Better or worse?

Ed   Take a wild guess.

She goes out.

Ed *winces with pain as he sits back on his haunches.*

Silence.

Well it's perfectly clear the NHS is not equipped to deal with male pregnancy. Where the fuck are the fucking doctors? Is it a *secret*? Have you seen a single doctor tonight? I shall write to the *Guardian*, they were spot on as usual, I take back everything I said.

He breathes out heavily, breathes in and out, trying to rest.

The alarm on the monitor sounds and **Lisa** *stares at the screen anxiously.*

Lisa   Oh, now what?

Ed   Oh, I'm going to complain.

Lisa (*studying it*)   You've been complaining for the last seven hours.

Ed   I'm a man it's my job – somebody's got to –

Lisa   Just don't make a scene – it's clearly making it worse.

Ed   It's my job to make a scene.

Lisa   Just don't burn your, you know, bridges –

Ed (*simultaneous with 'bridges'*)   Boats – bridges – mmn –

Lisa   If there's one thing you learn as a mother, it's endless fucking patience.

Ed   What you don't understand is I'm *hard wired* to go on the attack when I'm cornered. It's my responsibility to be antagonistic and kick up a stink and fuck with their heads and just generally, you know, get my own way. That's Darwinism. *You're* hard wired to tolerate everything.

Lisa   I'm just more patient than you.

Ed   I'm not *meant* to be patient – I'm meant to be *impatient*, keep them on their toes, push them around a bit, show them who's boss.

Lisa   Not while you're giving birth, it just doesn't work that way.

He hangs his head suddenly, back on his hands and knees, lets out a long, low, helpless moan.

Ed   Oh-I-feel-like-a-piece-of-meat! This is a nightmare a fucking unmitigated . . .

She watches him writhe in pain, becoming worried.

A young registrar, **Natasha**, *comes in with* **Joyce** *and looks at the monitor somewhat urgently.*

Natasha   Hi, I'm Natasha, I'm the registrar on tonight.

Lisa   Lisa and this is Ed.

Natasha   Hi.

Lisa   Hi.

Ed   Hi.

Natasha *approaches* **Ed***'s rear end, has a quick look, pulling on latex gloves with a snap.*

Natasha   How are you feeling?

Lisa   He's in a lot of pain.

Ed   I'm in a lot of pain.

Natasha   That's unusual. (*To* **Joyce**.) You need to change this sheet please. When was he last examined?

Joyce   I just examined him.

Lisa   It was hours ago.

Natasha   What time was it?

Joyce   It was about ten when he had a suppository.

Joyce *removes the sheet from the bed and disposes of it, replaces it with a fresh one.*

Lisa   He hasn't been examined properly yet.

Joyce   Yes I looked.

Lisa   No you didn't.

Joyce   Well, I did.

Lisa   Well, you didn't.

Joyce   I just did.

Lisa   You just *didn't*. Are you calling me a liar?

Joyce *bundles up the bed sheets and goes out.*

Natasha   He needs a scan. (*To* **Ed**.) Sit up properly please.

Ed *turns over painfully and sits up.*

Ed   I'm going to need a cushion down there . . . can you get a little . . . (*To* **Lisa**.) Like a little travelling cushion or something with a little hole in the middle? Like a doughnut? To sit on? A neck pillow I think that would be very –

Lisa   I'll see what I can do.

Natasha   Just hold still a minute.

Natasha *prepares the scanner, puts gel on* **Ed***'s belly, runs the scanner over it.*

Natasha *stares at the screen.*

Lisa *watches over her shoulder, anxious.*

Natasha *leans over and presses an alarm which sounds outside urgently as the heartbeat drops.*

Lisa   Is everything OK?

Pause.

Ed   Is the baby OK?

Natasha   She's actually moved.

Ed   I knew she had moved! We said she moved!

Lisa   What's wrong?

Natasha *studies the screen.*

Natasha   Looks like the cord's around her neck.

Ed   Oh, I knew it – I knew it – you just *know* don't you?

Natasha We have to remove the cord from around her neck as quickly as possible.

Ed Oh, I just want to know my baby's OK! Is my baby OK?

Natasha (*calls out*) Can I have some help in here!

She presses the call button.

We need to pop you up to theatre as quick as we can.

Joyce *comes in, comes over.*

Joyce Hello. How's it going?

Natasha (*taking off gloves*) The cord's around baby's neck and the heart rate's dropping.

Joyce Oh dear. It's a shame when that happens.

Natasha Do you know if theatre is free?

Joyce They've been very busy all night

Natasha Do you know if it's free now?

Joyce There's somebody in there now.

Natasha Do you know when they'll be out?

Joyce They only just went in . . .

Natasha What did they go in for?

Joyce I don't know . . .

Natasha Do you think you could find out?

Joyce OK I can try . . .

Natasha Tell them it's an emergency caesarean – quickly –

Joyce I'll leave you this.

Joyce *produces a tube of KY and hands it to* **Natasha**.

Natasha Where did you get the KY?

Joyce   I have a secret stash.

She goes out.

Natasha *throws away gloves.*

Natasha   Have you been given a painkiller?

Ed   I asked for an epidural hours ago.

Lisa   He's had Panadol.

Natasha   Well I think you're probably going to need something a bit stronger now.

Ed   Why?

Natasha   Because if we can't get up to theatre I'm going to try and get my hand in there to shift that cord from around the baby's neck. (**Ed** *stares.*) You'll need to turn over please. (**Ed** *stares.*) Hello? Turn over, my love, that's the way . . .

Ed (*shifting, appalled*)   Oh I can't bear it I just can't bear it any longer!

Ed *awkwardly turns over.*

Natasha *produces another pair of latex gloves.*

What's happening? What are you doing?

Natasha   I have to move it down and away from the bowel in case there's a rupture.

Lisa   Oh my God.

Natasha   It's very common in male pregnancies. If the placenta has fused against the bowel wall . . .

Lisa   My God . . .

Natasha   It could be another reason he's in so much pain.

Pulling on latex gloves.

This might hurt a bit.

Ed   I want my epidural!

Natasha   Go on, a strapping lad like you?

Ed I asked for it hours ago!

Natasha You'll be fine.

Natasha *slathers a large amount of KY on her gloved hands and wrists.*

Ed What's happening? What are you . . .?

Lisa She's going to turn the baby – they had to turn Charlie – it's normal.

Ed 'Normal'? What about *this* is normal?

Natasha Don't worry. It's more flexible than you think down there . . . (*She stares, quiet, concentrates.*) Everything will spring back – we'll give you exercises –

Ed Exercises!

Natasha Try not to clench – just be as relaxed as you can – it won't hurt at all if you can stay loose and just relax your muscles . . . it's much better I do this now than later . . .

Ed Do I get a choice?

Natasha You can wait for theatre and have a general anaesthetic but I don't want to wait – I don't recommend any more delay –

Ed *Please* wait for theatre –

Natasha I don't know how long we could be waiting –

Ed Wait for theatre! I want to wait!

Natasha You'll have your C-section when theatre is free but right now I have to turn the foetus and dislodge this cord quickly or the placenta could haemorrhage.

Ed What are they doing in there? This is insane.

Natasha We've had a lot of emergencies tonight.

Ed *This* is an emergency!

Joyce *comes back in.*

Natasha (*to* **Joyce**)   Tell them we need some help getting ready for theatre and get ready to start moving him out please . . .

Joyce   OK . . .

Natasha   And you need to take the tap out please . . .

Joyce *takes out the catheter, talking to* **Lisa**.

Joyce   Could you pack all your bags up now please?

Joyce *starts dismantling the drip –* **Natasha** *notices her struggling with the drip.*

Natasha   Take the tap out of his arm quickly please.

Joyce   I've been trying, I screwed it too tightly I think.

Natasha   Well it's got to come out now.

Joyce (*trying to remove it again*)   I don't know my own strength

Lisa   Don't bruise him.

Joyce (*to* **Lisa**)   Pick up all the clothes and get ready to move out – quickly – yes now – now.

She accidentally breaks the tap of the drip off.

Oh no, that's a shame.

Lisa   Careful!

Ed   Are you insane? Are you doing it on purpose?

Joyce *continues to fiddle with the broken tap from the drip in* **Ed**'s *arm, yanking it around but unable to remove it.*

Ed *watches in pain.*

Joyce   I just don't understand it. (*Regarding drip.*) I'm sorry he's bleeding quite badly . . .

Natasha   Just let me do that.

Lisa   Will you be finishing your shift any time soon? Surely there's another midwife.

Natasha *takes the bloodied tap and drip out of* **Ed**'s *arm neatly and easily, throws it in the sharps bin.*

An alarm sounds in the distance.

Go and get some help moving this bed please now please.

Joyce *goes out.*

Ed *puts a hand on* **Natasha**'s *arm.*

Ed   What are the risks here?

Natasha   Where, what do you mean?

Ed   What are the risks of a caesar?

Natasha   Well there's risks with everything.

Ed   Yes but I heard of all these *risks* with surgery.

Natasha   Crossing the street is a risk.

Ed   Infection? Blood loss? Bowel problems?

Natasha   Did you go to your NCT classes?

Ed   They don't tell you anything.

Natasha   They tell you everything.

Ed   No they don't.

Natasha   Did you sign a waiver? You would have signed a form –

Ed   I changed –

Natasha   When you arrived –

Ed   Yes but –

Natasha   Saying yes –

Ed   But I've –

Natasha   To the surgery.

Ed   I've changed my mind. I can't go through with it.

Lisa   Eddie . . . please . . .

Natasha (*amused*)   You can't change your mind now.

Ed   Can't you do anything else?

Natasha   There really is no other way this baby is coming out. Now put your head down and just . . . brace yourself . . .

He changes position, head down, groaning worriedly.

Lots of gas and air now . . .

Lisa *hands* **Ed** *the gas, he takes gas and air, round-eyed and silent now.*

Big breaths . . .

Ed *gulps it down while* **Lisa** *clears up their things and* **Natasha** *starts pulling IVs away from the bed, preparing to move it.*

Head down that's right and push backwards towards me please . . .

Natasha *places both hands on* **Ed**'s *buttocks.*

Ed *braces himself against her.*

Push backwards hard . . .

Ed *pushes.*

And here we go . . .

Ed (*gritting his teeth, anticipating*)   It's like a bad dream . . .! Three two one relax –

Lisa (*joining in*)   Three two one relax . . . three two one relax . . .

Natasha *is about to insert her fingers into* **Ed**'s *anus when* **Joyce** *comes back.*

Joyce   OK I've spoken to the surgeon he says the theatre is free now.

Natasha (*pausing*)   When did they finish?

Joyce   Just finished. They're writing up their notes.

Natasha Eddie?

Ed What?

Natasha It's your lucky day.

She tugs his gown down to conceal his rump and gives him a friendly pat on the bottom.

She presses the call button and it sounds in the distance, adding to the general clamour.

Natasha *and* **Joyce** *grab the end of the bed with determination.*

Let's roll him out . . .

They push and pull the bed out through the door.

Lisa *just stands there a second, somewhat stunned, in the middle of packing, she quickly finishes and rushes out after them.*

Blackout.

Act Two

Scene One

6 a.m. Saturday.

Ed *lies propped up on the bed in a bloody gown, connected to a morphine drip.*

He is motionless, drowsy.

Lisa *is sitting on the bed, sleepless and dishevelled.*

Silence.

Lisa   Could you believe that shit with the table?

They couldn't even get the operating table up . . .

Ed   I seemed to be lying there for hours with my bits dangling about against the chrome . . . all sorts of draughts wafting this way and that while they fussed about with the handles . . .

Lisa   That's exactly what happened to me.

Ed   It was probably the same table.

Lisa   It was, it was the exact same table. They had two anaesthetists – *two* in the end – nothing for hours and hours then suddenly – like buses . . . they had *two* surgeons, a football team of nurses and nobody could unfold the stupid bloody fucking table . . .

Ed   How long did it take to put me under?

Lisa   It took a few goes.

Ed   I think I was tripping. Tripping on ketamine probably. I still feel quite trippy now . . .

Lisa   You'd think they'd be ready for you. You'd think that as a man you could *book* it – *book* your caesarean. It should have been *scheduled*, a *scheduled* . . . the whole thing was just . . . (*Trails off.*) They just want us to piss off and go private.

Ed   Well anyway, I really need you to try and stay positive now . . . (*He holds her hand.*) I want this to be a positive experience from now on, focus on the . . . you know . . . I'm trying not to become demoralised.

She grips his hand, strokes his head.

Lisa   Watching you lying there opened up like a science project, completely lifeless while they cut you open . . . watching them put you under was like watching them put you to *death*. It was like a a a *death camp*.

Ed   That's really helping, Lisa. Upgraded from 'veal crate' to 'death camp'.

Lisa   I'm sorry . . .

She digs in her bag for her bag of crisps, she offers the bag and he snatches it, eats, ravenous.

I've had a complete sense of humour failure. It's such a fine line between optimism and despair. I think we're both a lot more vulnerable than we realised.

Ed (*picking his teeth, mouth full*)   Yeah, vulnerable, absolutely, I'm incredibly vulnerable . . .

He belches, screws up the empty bag, looks for a place to throw it, throws it on the floor.

Natasha *comes in with* **Ed**'*s notes.*

Natasha   Hello.

Lisa   Hello.

Natasha   How are you feeling?

Lisa   Good . . .

Ed (*simultaneous*)   OK . . .

Natasha   A bit sore?

Ed   Bit tender mm . . .

Natasha   You'll have a bit of a scar but I'm sure you don't mind . . .

Ed   Oh, it's pretty hairy down there . . . I don't think it's going to really . . . (*Trails off.*)

Natasha   How's your bum? (*No reply.*) It's always very difficult for men when they have these things done to them. It's very humiliating for them. They feel violated. They have such different expectations of life.

Natasha *looks at his notes.*

I'm sorry you were left on your own for so long. Healthy people with no problems tend to be left alone to get on with it so all the other staff can be diverted to the emergencies . . . it's all very carefully *rationed* . . . everybody gets enough, just enough, to keep them alive . . .

Lisa   But that midwife just seemed to be – if you don't mind me saying – completely –

Natasha   Hm –

Lisa   Stupid and –

Natasha   It's true, it's not rocket science –

Lisa   Bovine.

Natasha   Well . . . it was a busy night . . . lots going on . . . loads of men last night . . . you probably heard all the shouting . . . men are hard work. You always hear them when they come in. They bring their mums. They bring their boyfriends and make a party of it. (*To* **Lisa**.) It's a big deal for them, d'you know what I mean? (*To* **Ed**.) Has your boyfriend been to visit you yet?

Ed (*beat*)   Eh?

Natasha   Has your partner seen the baby?

Ed (*beat*)   Yes – this is my . . .

Natasha   Oh your . . .? I'm sorry, I thought you were just the 'advocate'.

Lisa   No, I'm just the 'wife', he's my husband, it's complicated, I understand.

Natasha   It's quite unusual for a married man to . . . (*Trails off.*) Unless there's a pretty good reason . . . I appreciate that it's a very private . . .

Ed   I'm heterosexual.

Natasha   It's none of my business . . .

Lisa   He really is. Completely heterosexual . . .

Natasha   Absolutely, I understand that now . . .

She studies her notes, writes something.

Lisa   When can we see the baby?

Natasha   We're just waiting for the results of her blood test.

Ed   Is everything all right?

Natasha   Everything's fine but the first set of results showed a very high antibody so I wanted to do it again.

Ed   High antibody? What does that mean?

Natasha   It means the white blood cell count was very low.

Lisa   That's bad, right?

Natasha   Either the test was tainted or if it's accurate she'll need antibiotics.

Natasha *checks the IV, tries to clear an air bubble.*

Lisa   Where is she now?

Natasha   She's in the high-dependency unit – it sounds worse than it is but it's nothing to worry about.

Lisa   Nobody told us this.

Natasha   I just told you.

Ed   Is she all right?

Natasha   She has a slight temperature but it's nothing to worry about . . .

Lisa   What's her temperature?

Natasha   It's a hundred and four but it's nothing to worry about . . . What we usually do is get an IV in and put them on antibiotics for forty-eight hours to fight off any infection.

Ed   I don't want her on antibiotics.

Natasha *ignores him, studies the drip in his arm.*

She taps it to get rid of air.

Lisa   What sort of infection?

Natasha   It's just a precaution – if there's a negative reaction we'll take her straight off them again.

Ed   I've read terrible things about antibiotics they'll strip her stomach of all the natural – she'll get a yeast infection . . .

Natasha   They're very mild and if there's any –

Ed   No but you don't understand when she comes out – later *later* – this is what happened to our son Charlie – he was on antibiotics and he got terrible stomach cramps and he basically –

Lisa   Don't panic –

Ed   You don't understand!

Lisa   You're not listening – listen to her –

Natasha   It's quite safe if you don't want us to.

Ed   Well I don't.

Natasha   We would take her off them if there was –

Ed   I don't want you to.

Natasha   You don't want to try them at all? So that's a No? From *both* of you?

Ed   Yes, it's a No. I think I've made myself clear. No. From both of us.

They all look at each other.

Natasha (*to* **Ed**, *soothingly*)   Just a minute, my love, I just need to talk to your partner for a sec. (*Deferring to* **Lisa**.) What are you thinking?

Lisa   I don't know . . .

Natasha   We need to establish whether she has a secondary infection – which is actively killing her white blood cells – or whether she started life with a low count anyway.

Ed (*eavesdropping*)   So it's all *her* fault?

Lisa   Ed, just relax, you're not helping, everybody's doing their best . . . (*To* **Natasha**.) I'm saying Yes. If you need my permission.

Ed   *Your* permission? *You're* giving permission? For both of us?

Lisa   I'm still the mother.

Ed   And I'm the father – I'm the boss!

Lisa   You're not 'the boss'.

Ed   *And* I'm a mother *too*. In a, in a very real sense –

Lisa   I'm the *advocate* – I'm your *advocate* – I'm allowed to make decisions without –

Ed   No you should *consult* we need to consult –

Lisa   I made an *executive decision*.

Ed   But you're *not qualified*. How do you know what to do?!

Lisa   Because I've done it before.

Ed   And you'll never let me forget that will you? You *always* do this: you make the decisions for me!

Lisa   That's because you take for ever.

Ed   Well I just like to consider all the options and be sure.

Lisa   Well I just need you to chill out a bit now.

Ed   I am chilled – I'm completely chilled.

Lisa   Just calm down.

Ed   I am calm – I'm fucking calm – so just shut up about it!

Natasha (*to* **Ed**)   OK, my love, just . . . try not to get upset. Have a glass of water.

Natasha *pours* **Ed** *a glass of water and hands it to him as she talks to* **Lisa**.

Perhaps he'd like a magazine to look at?

Lisa   We just want to see our baby now.

Natasha   I'll be honest with you: we need to eliminate the possibility of a staph infection.

Lisa   'Staph'?

Natasha   Staphylococcal.

Lisa   Oh Christ . . .

Ed   What does that mean?

Natasha   It's just a systemic hospital infection, it happens all the time, don't worry . . .

Lisa   OK . . . but . . . wait . . . on the spectrum of hospital infections it's a, what, it's a . . .? If you were to rate it from one to ten?

Natasha   Well look, staph is a very invasive infection so her blood pressure might drop and she may experience some swelling . . . and if we don't treat it properly it can in theory lead to a blood clot or organ failure in tiny babies . . . but we don't know if it's staph yet, it's very unlikely . . .

Ed *and* **Lisa** *stare, shocked*.

The *good* news is that we've caught it early and if it responds to antibiotics we can treat it here and now, and she'll go home in a week.

Ed *and* **Lisa** *fall quiet*.

Put it this way, if she's going to catch some sort of nasty infection then this is the place to catch it.

Pause.

Ed   And and and what if it doesn't respond to antibiotics . . .? What's the the the the the the bad news?

Natasha   If it's a bacterium that's resistant to antibiotics then we say it's 'meticillin resistant . . .' and we find another way of treating it.

Lisa   So then it's, it's, it's MRSA . . .? Like a, like a *superbug* . . .?

Natasha   Comme ci comme ça.

Lisa   It is or it isn't.

Natasha   We should cross that bridge when we come to it.

Lisa   We *have* come to it. When will we know?

Natasha   Soon.

Ed   Oh, I can't bear it any longer – I feel nauseous, I'm going to be sick – I really just can't *cope any more!*

Lisa   Ed – please – just – pull yourself together now. I'm sorry – he's not really . . .

Natasha   Do you think he'd like a valium? It'll calm him down.

Lisa   He'll be fine in a moment. I really think we need the consultant now.

Natasha   Hasn't he been down yet?

Ed   No he has not 'been down'. He hasn't condescended yet to 'be down . . .' I suppose I'm not important enough . . . just another silly man who's got himself up the duff . . .

Lisa *and* **Natasha** *eye him uncertainly.*

Lisa   Doesn't he have ward rounds?

Ed   He's probably on the fucking golf course.

Natasha   Well, it's the weekend . . .

Ed   The weekend! These idiots . . . are *idiots*!

Natasha   I'll make sure he has a look at her as soon as he can.

Lisa   Can we see him?

Natasha   Sure, I'll make sure he comes to see you too.

Lisa   Because you can understand how we're feeling about this . . .

Natasha   It's not ideal. But consultant or no consultant it's my responsibility and I will personally commit myself to this now. I'll organise an antifungal to go with the antibiotics and I'll put the IV in myself with my own fair hands.

Lisa   Thank you, Natasha . . . can I call you Natasha?

Natasha   Of course you can. (*To* **Ed**.) Now, have you had a blood test?

Ed   Not yet. Why?

Natasha   You're looking a bit peaky. Poor old thing. Just let me go and find a nurse.

She takes off her gloves etc.

It's lucky you caught me. I was just about to go home.

She smiles and goes out.

Silence.

Lisa *takes tissues from a box and hands them to* **Ed** – *he blows his nose, teary.*

She holds him in her arms tenderly, strokes his face, caresses and comforts him.

Lisa   Shh . . . it's all right . . . I'm here . . . I'm here now. Don't worry . . . don't worry . . . dig deep sweetie, come on, not long to go now, nearly there, you've been so brave, you really are very, very brave . . .

She kisses him tenderly on the face and head, dries his tears with a tissue.

Joyce *comes in.* **Lisa** *checks her texts.*

Joyce Sit up please. I need to check your stitches.

Ed When does your shift end? Couldn't you swap with someone?

Joyce I'm doing a double shift so you've got me for a little bit longer.

Ed Aren't you tired? You're too tired.

Joyce Pffft . . .

Lisa I'd better get home for a couple of hours, Mum says Charlie's starting to lose it. Is there anything you want? Beer? Cornish pasty? A *Guardian*?

Ed I don't care any more . . . whatever . . . I'm not hungry . . .

She eyes him worriedly and goes out.

Ed *eyes* **Joyce** *uncertainly as she washes her hands busily with antiseptic soap.*

Joyce What are you looking at? Tsk. Nobody wants the African midwife. Everybody thinks African midwives are so rough and tough. We think Anglo Saxons are very soft and you cry too much. Why are you so unhappy? Babies are *life*. Babies replace the dead. Cheer up. Lift your top.

He lifts his top, eyes her nervously.

I think you are afraid of Africans.

Ed Not at all . . . I love Africans . . . some of my best friends are Africans . . .

She lifts his shirt further, feels his glands, neck, under arms, he squirms.

Joyce You are ticklish . . .

Ed   No . . .

Joyce (*tickling*)   You are . . .

Ed   No . . .

Joyce   Is that nice? (*Tickling.*) Tickle-ickle . . .

Ed   Get off . . .

Joyce   You're so skinny . . . you're like a bird . . .

Ed   I've put on a stone, it's embarrassing . . .

Joyce   Tsk. You are as delicate and thin as a little girl. My husband would never put up with you . . .

Ed   I eat too much chocolate. My wife doesn't approve . . .

Joyce   She doesn't want you to let yourself go. She wants you to have a nice firm little bottom to smack just like a boy.

Ed   I wish! Actually I think she quite likes me, you know, quite curvy. Gives her something to get hold of . . .

Joyce   Have a couple more and then see what she says. I have seven children and I think I might be pregnant again.

Ed   Really? You wouldn't know it . . .

Joyce (*gives him a look*)   Tsk . . . you're cheeky.

She examines the stitches in his abdomen, prods, frowning.

Joyce   Hmm . . . hmmm . . . hmm . . . hm . . . hmmmmm . . . mm . . . mm . . . uh . . .

Ed   What's wrong?

Joyce   This is very puffy.

Ed   'Puffy'?

Joyce   *Puffy*, the scar, puffed up. How are you feeling?

Ed   A bit knocked about . . .

Joyce   Are you feeling fluey or achy?

Ed   A bit yeah . . .

Joyce   Hmm. (*Looking closer.*) It's very oozy.

Ed   'Oozy'?

Joyce   Oozing a bit of blood still. It's not good when they don't stop bleeding. Is it itchy?

Ed   N . . . yeah now you mention it . . .

Joyce   Hmm. (*To herself.*) Puffy itchy oozy fluey . . . puffy itchy oozy fluey . . .

Joyce *dabs at the stitches with cotton wool, frowns, dabs again.*

Are you a haemophiliac?

Ed   No. Why?

Joyce   I don't understand why it's still oozing.

She checks his arm.

You're very bruised. I think you might have a condition which is quite conducive to a lot of bleeding, it's not the same as haemophilia, what it is basically is very thin skin.

Ed   I have thin skin?

Joyce (*dabbing doubtfully*)   Mmmm . . .

Ed   That's your diagnosis is it, your expert medical opinion?

Joyce   You're very pale still, have you ever been anaemic?

Ed   Anaemic? No.

Joyce   Do you take an iron supplement?

Ed   During my pregnancy.

Joyce   White people always look pale in hospital . . . it's the fluorescent lighting. I always look very black at work.

I'm naturally quite black anyway – the backs of my knees are very, very black – but something about a hospital accentuates

it. Let me take your blood pressure. We don't want you
fainting when you get up to go to the toilet . . . we don't want
you passing out and squashing the baby flat.

*She readies the equipment, puts the cuff around his arm, measures
systolic pressure.*

OK, your blood pressure is very low. I think this is infected. I
would like the doctor to have another look at you.

Ed   She just saw me, I'm fine. She just checked me, I'm
fine. I'm absolutely fine . . . aren't I?

Blackout.

Scene Two

Saturday evening.

Ed *silent, eating chocolates.*

Lisa *has unpacked a bag of shopping, drinks, sandwiches,
magazines, box of chocolates.*

Ed   Did you manage to get me that cushion to sit on? The
little doughnut-shaped . . . I'll need it when we get home . . .

Lisa   I searched and searched . . .

Ed   There must be something. An inner tube – use your
brains . . .

Lisa   I'll look again . . .

Ed   A travelling cushion or something – a neck pillow –

Lisa   They just don't make that sort of thing for men –

Ed   Have you tried Mothercare? Try Halfords they're
usually pretty –

Lisa   Yes – I tried everybody –

Ed   Look on the internet have you tried Amazon?

Lisa   I'm trying –

Ed   Well you're not trying hard enough.

Lisa   Ed I'm sorry you're in so much pain, I'm trying my best . . .

Ed   Well think about it . . .

Lisa   I'm wracking my brains . . .

Ed   I feel as if I'm doing all the work here.

Lisa   *I'm* doing all the work! *I'm* doing it! I've been rushing around for nine months, fetching and carrying for you, while you loaf about *eating*. I'm like your *butler.*

Ed   I'm sorry if I'm *inconveniencing* you –

Lisa   I've been trying to help Mum with Charlie and calm him down because he doesn't understand where you are and he's becoming very – I'm just tired –

Ed (*simultaneous with 'tired'*)   Oh 'tired'. And that makes it OK . . .

Lisa   Could you just stop snapping?

Ed (*simultaneous with 'snapping'*)   Just pull your finger out.

Lisa   For God's sake – you're so *controlling*.

Ed   I am not 'controlling'. I forbid you to use that word. I *forbid* you to call me 'controlling'!

Lisa   I wasn't like this when Charlie was born.

Ed   You have no concept whatsoever of the pain.

Lisa   I have *some* concept.

Ed   Of *my* pain – male pain – *man pain*. You've no idea how difficult this is.

Lisa   O-ho, I think I *do*.

Ed   You don't understand and you never will unless you grow a penis.

Lisa   *I'm going to.*

Ed   This shouldn't happen to a man. It's just not fair.

Lisa   But it should happen to a *woman*? Because it's quote unquote 'normal' for a woman. Which bit of it do you think feels *normal* for a woman? You're lucky you didn't wind up in stirrups!

Ed   Don't deliberately twist everything – we were told it shouldn't happen the way it happened with *you* is what I meant . . .

Lisa   You're lucky it didn't.

Ed   Everything's different with a man. It's far more complicated . . . *psychologically* . . . *existentially* . . .

Lisa   It's not a *lobotomy* . . .

Ed   It's so *emasculating* . . .

Lisa   You're just frightened. I'm frightened too. It's frightening. But you're beginning to sound like you *regret* it.

Silence.

Lisa *puts everything back in the bag.*

Ed   I just need some tenderness. You never say you love me any more.

Lisa   You never say you love *me* any more.

Ed   Because I am busy having our baby!

Lisa   No, I think you *use* this as an excuse –

Ed   How could I use *this*?

Lisa   To be bolshy and rude and neurotic –

Ed   I'm not neurotic – you always say that – it's so *sexist*. I should never have let you bully me into this. Just don't bother waiting for me to come home after all this is over because I won't, I'll just go and stay at my mum's . . .

Lisa   Now you're just being silly . . .

Ed   And I'll tell her how *mean* you've been to me . . .

Lisa   You are completely –

Ed (*simultaneous*)   No –

Lisa   Hys –

Ed   No –

Lisa   Hyst –

Ed   I am not –

Lisa   Hysterical!

Ed (*simultaneous*)   Hysterical!

Lisa   I can't go back to *my* mum! We have two children now!

Ed   Oh, just stop playing with my *emotions*! You're so *manipulative*!

Lisa   Oh *fuck off*.

Ed   I wish I could.

Lisa   I wish you could too.

Ed   Or *you* could.

Lisa   I wish I could too!

Ed   Then go! Leave me holding the baby!

Lisa   I will if you're not careful!

Ed   And then I'll divorce you and I'll keep the house and I'll get –

Lisa   Bring it on –

Ed   Custody –

Lisa   Divorce me, I'm waiting, I'm ready!

Ed   You stupid *bitch*! Are you happy now?

Lisa   No! Are you?

Joyce *comes in.*

Joyce   Hello how are you doing? I've come to look at your scar.

They all pretend there's been no argument as she examines **Ed**.

Mm, this is looking better . . .

Ed (*apropos of nothing*)   They say tea tree oil's very good for scars . . . just a couple of drops in the, in the bath . . .

Lisa   I'll fetch you some on the way home . . .

Joyce *rubs in cream.*

Joyce   I will give you this cream to take with you. It has a steroid for the puffiness and an antibiotic for the infection. It's very good. It's very nice . . .

Joyce *finishes and goes out again.*

Ed   It's just the worry. It's the worry. What's going to happen to her? I just want to go home . . . I can't spend another night in this place waiting . . . it's so noisy and smelly and stuffy . . . I've been tossing and turning . . . I haven't had a wink of sleep. I get so lonely in here all on my own. I just want to sleep in my own bed . . . I want a nice hot bath . . . with some nice bath salts . . . and scented candles. I just want my life back.

Lisa   I felt exactly the same when Charlie was born. I thought I'd never get out of hospital. It's a miracle when they make it out alive – an even *bigger* miracle when you make it out of hospital.

Ed   She's in an incubator filling up on antibiotics I never asked for, fighting an infection she never asked for, I'm lying here 'oozing' like a *spayed tabby* – which part of that is a miracle? It's a 'miracle' I haven't strangled anybody!

Lisa   Don't say that. You're starting to sound mad.

Ed   Well I am now.

He grunts and picks up the first thing to hand – the sharps bin full of discarded needles – flings it across the room.

Look at me: I've gone insane! My mind is blown . . . my nerves are in shreds . . . Eh? Can they help me with any of these issues? If anything happens to her I'll go down to the cottage and borrow a gun off a farmer –

Lisa   Don't say that –

Ed   Borrow a shotgun and start –

Lisa   You have a beautiful son –

Ed   Shooting people . . .

Lisa   You've gone to the dark side.

Ed   And then I'll shoot myself.

Lisa   You've just lost control.

Ed   Because I just want to die.

Lisa   You don't want to die.

Ed   Yes I do.

He impotently yanks at the IV in his arm, generally thrashes about as he continues.

I wanted to die when we couldn't have babies when you had all the miscarriages, I wanted to die when we were having Charlie and you were in here in the same bed and I thought you were going to die and I thought he was going to die, I wanted to die after you had him and you couldn't have any more we couldn't sleep he couldn't sleep he was always sick . . . and now it feels like we're back at square one 'Go back to the start do not pass Go do not collect 200 pounds go straight to THE END OF YOUR TETHER' – it just seems to get . . . *exponentially* . . . (*Gestures, futile.*) Everybody's always so platitudinous and insincere. Thanking God and all that shit. Nobody ever tells the *truth* about it because that's *against nature*. To privately think it isn't worth it – it's *taboo*. And even if it *is* worth it, the cost is just so . . . *disproportionately* . . . (*Trails off, pause.*) Do we *know* any farmers?

Lisa   You'll forget. You will forget about all this. Children heal you. Children take away the pain.

Ed   Do they 'take away the pain' of having children?

Lisa   I was exactly the same, then suddenly it all . . . you
bounce back and everything goes away and . . . everybody
has a choice to move on or or or dwell on all this negativity
and *farm* the *scars*. Look at me now: I love being a mother
. . . I see the world through his eyes . . . I'm remembering
my childhood – I'm reliving my childhood –

Ed   I don't want to relive my childhood.

Lisa   No but I live each new day with the vividness and
intensity of a child.

Ed   I don't want things to be intense. They're already
intense.

Lisa   All the pain and misery and worry and pressure from
before is completely . . . it's evaporated . . . and I'm
transformed . . . don't you agree? (*He just stares, blankly.*) You
can't see it now because you've obviously got a touch of
post-natal . . . you're just a bit depressed because we don't
know what's going to happen and we're still lost in the void
but . . . it's just hormones.

Ed   It is not the fucking hormones! Stop talking about
hormones! They've exploited our goodwill and sacrificed
our equanimity!

Lisa (*pause, quietly*)   Well, I don't know what to say when
you're like this. What do you want?

Ed (*ripping out IV*)   I want *revenge*!

He throws the IV to the floor.

I have a *brain*!

He rips up the bed, throws all the bedding to the floor.

I have an *intellect*!

Natasha *appears at the door, he doesn't notice.*

He trashes the room violently.

I'm fucking *sensitive*!

Natasha *comes in, surveys the mess.*

Natasha   Would you like that valium now?

Lisa   Yes please.

Silence.

Natasha   The good news is the baby's responding to antibiotics, her temperature's come down and there's no evidence of staph, so you should go home in a few days.

Pause.

Ed   Uh . . .

Lisa   Thank God!

Ed   Oh I'm so relieved I'm –

Lisa   I'm just so –

Ed   I'm –

Lisa   I'm –

Ed   I mean my God! Wa-hey!

Lisa   Fuck! Shit!

Ed   Cunt! (*To* **Natasha**.) Thank you, I could kiss you! You're so clever! You're a genius!

Lisa   We're going home!

Ed   I'm so happy! I've never been so fucking happy in my life! What did I tell you? These people are geniuses!

Blackout.

Scene Three

A few days later.

Tidy room, large bunches of roses, lilies, tulips and sunflowers all around with cards.

Lisa *is dressed up, doing her make-up,* **Natasha** *is wearing headphones around her neck and an iPod, drinking a cup of coffee and sporadically writing up notes.*

Natasha   I wouldn't have a natural birth if you put a gun to my head. Fuck that for a bunch of bananas. One of the most dangerous, chaotic, stressful things a woman can do. I wouldn't subject my worst enemy to it let alone somebody I loved because, basically, you're playing *Russian roulette*. (*Pause.*) Obstetrics is the most stressful job you can do. I wanted to be a gynaecologist but I couldn't bear the politics – it's a man's world, gynaecology.

Pause as she writes.

Lisa   Do you have kids?

Natasha   No, not for me. My boyfriend wants one but after everything I've seen . . . no chance, I'm not risking it. He can have it himself. I'll hold his hand.

Lisa   Don't you want kids?

Natasha   I don't have any maternal instinct. I don't have a maternal bone in my body. Children annoy me a bit to be honest . . . they're so selfish and distracting . . . how can you concentrate? (*Pause, writing.*) I feel a bit sorry for people with children . . . I can't relate to them . . . I see them come in here with their bags packed, all worried and excited, as if they're setting off on some incredible voyage . . . to a strange new world . . . but they're never coming home.

Lisa   I used to think it would be the easiest thing imaginable . . . I used to think any old idiot could do it . . .

As she says this, the toilet flushes and **Ed** *emerges from the bathroom doing up his trousers, dressed in his ordinary clothes, self-absorbed, somewhat recovered, toilet paper emerging from the back of his trousers.*

Ed   I piss like a horse. I have silent farts.

He straightens the bed a bit.

Lisa (*retrieving toilet paper*)   Hang on. Let me help . . .

Lisa *abandons her make-up and straightens the bed.*

Ed *starts packing a little bag with his things – medication mostly.*

Joyce *comes in.*

Joyce   Ready to go?

Ed   Hi, yes . . .

Joyce   Have you been doing your exercises?

Ed   Every day.

Joyce   Don't forget to clench. (*Mimes 'clenching'.*)

Ed   I have been. Like my life depends on it.

Joyce   Strengthens your core.

Ed   Where's the car?

Lisa   I found a visitors' bay.

Ed   Give me the keys.

She hands him the car keys.

He puts on a jumper, smooths his hair, preparing to go.

Joyce   I'll go and get the baby, she's with the other midwives.

Lisa   I'm so excited . . .

Joyce   She needs a feed so I will fetch you some formula . . .

Joyce *goes.*

Ed *gets a bottle ready.*

Natasha   I'll do it, you finish packing.

*He hands **Natasha** the bottle etc. and she goes out.*

Ed *finishes packing.*

Lisa *watches him fondly.*

Lisa   I'm so proud of you . . .

Ed   I'm proud of myself. (*Becoming self-conscious.*) How do I look?

Lisa   You look nice.

Ed   Do I look fat? Don't look at me. I've got a muffin top.

Lisa   How do I look?

Ed (*packing*)   You look nice, mm.

Lisa   I splashed out. For work. Do you like it?

He looks up.

Ed   Uh?

Lisa   Do you like my hair?

Ed   Great.

Lisa   I had my nails done too I treated myself –

Ed (*eyeing her*)   I'd forgotten how . . . I'd forgotten how . . .

She turns around.

She strikes a pose and he really notices.

Do that again.

She poses, revealing her legs.

Wow. What's got into you, what have you been doing?

She touches him tenderly.

Lisa   We need to become the people we were before. Before all this, before babies – when we met, when we got married, before we knew anything about – any of this – those people. Remember those people?

Ed   Yes. I liked those people.

Lisa   We need to be young again.

Ed   How?

Lisa   I don't know how.

Ed   Is there some sort of, of *procedure*?

Lisa   I want to try without medical intervention this time.

Ed   I want to too.

She kisses him tenderly.

Lisa   We don't have to go through it ever again.

Ed   I don't want to – no – never.

Lisa   We have everything we need now and we're happy.

Ed   We did it.

Lisa   We're a family.

Ed   We're finished.

Lisa   We're complete and I love you.

Ed   I love you too – I adore – I love everybody.

They hear the distinctive cry of a newborn baby, bawling, hungry, coming closer along the corridor.

Lisa   Listen.

They listen.

Ed   The music of life.

Lisa   Are you ready?

Ed   We haven't thought of a name.

Lisa   I've got one.

Ed   Tell me.

Blackout.